Speaking
inTongues

Speaking in Tongues

Initial Evidence of Spirit Baptism?

John A. Lombard Jr.
Jerald J. Daffe

Pathway PRESS

Book Editor: Wanda Griffith
Editorial Assistant: Tammy Hatfield
Copy Editor: Esther Metaxas
Julie E. McGuire

Library of Congress Catalog Card Number: 2005927048
ISBN: 1-59684-079-X
Copyright 2005 Pathway Press
Cleveland, Tennessee 37311

Other Pathway titles by these authors:

Dr. John A. Lombard, Jr.
Speaking for God

Dr. Jerald J. Daffe
In the Face of Evil

Life Challenges for Men

Revival: God's Plan for His People

*Minister's Service Manual
for Contemporary Church Celebrations*

DEDICATED

to our fathers,

Reverend John A. Lombard Sr.

and the late

Reverend John H. Daffe

who instilled in us a
love for God's Word
while faithfully
living and preaching
in the power of
God's Spirit.

CONTENTS

Acknowledgments 11

Foreword 13

Introduction 15

Part I
Prophetic Preparation

1. Empowered Leadership 19
   Old Testament Examples
   Old Testament Prophecies

2. The Holy Spirit in the Life and
   Ministry of Jesus 35

3. Jesus' Prophetic Preparation for
   His Disciples 45

Part II
Biblical Fulfillment

4. Baptism in the Holy Spirit 59
   Conviction, Regeneration, Sanctification
   Distinct Experience

5. Speaking in Tongues 77

6. Living in the Spirit 95

Part III
Historical Evidence

7. Montanist to the Shakers 113

8. Irvingites to the Parhamites 131

9. Azusa to the Present 147

Part IV
Reappearing Issues

10. Persistent Concerns 175

11. Perspective 195

Part V
Spirit Fullness

12. Receiving the Baptism of the
    Holy Spirit 211

ACKNOWLEDGMENTS

We express our appreciation to

Alisa L. Nelson

and

Jessica L. Davenport

for typing the manuscript
for the book.

FOREWORD

The apostle Paul wrote, "I wish you all spoke with tongues" (1 Corinthians 14:4, *NKJV*). This positive desire of the apostle has attracted the attention of more than 600 million believers who teach and practice the fullness of the Holy Spirit with the evidence of speaking in tongues.

The Pentecostal/Charismatic/Renewal stream of Christian movements is the largest and fastest-growing segment of the church in the world today. Although many factors may help explain the rapid expansion of these churches, the most prominent difference between these and other churches is their insistence on the need for the baptism in the Holy Spirit.

Speaking in Tongues: Initial Evidence of Spirit Baptism?, by John Lombard Jr. and Jerald Daffe, does not claim to be an exhaustive study of this vital doctrine, but it is an excellent introduction to those who wish to understand the Biblical understanding and belief posture of the major Pentecostal movements.

The book underlines a clear distinction: Salvation and baptism in the Holy Spirit are not the same thing. Some aberrant Pentecostal offshoots assert that it is necessary to speak in tongues in order to be saved, but the Bible does not make this claim. The purposes and benefits of speaking in tongues will be apparent to readers of this book.

I commend *Speaking in Tongues* to earnest-hearted seekers who wish to learn from the Bible and the experience of believers across the ages what God wants us to know about this significant doctrine. The authors' inclusion of a study guide at the end of each chapter makes it a valuable resource for those who wish to make it the basis of a formal study.

—G. Dennis McGuire
General Overseer
Church of God

INTRODUCTION

In general, believers are positive toward the need for revival and spiritual renewal. The thought of drawing closer to God and experiencing the dynamics of divine intervention is appealing. It seems, however, a vast majority do not realize how a crisis of faith and practice, which necessitates renewal, may come from faulty or neglected doctrinal foundations.

When we study the Great Awakening of the 1700s and read of Jonathan Edward's sermon "Sinners in the Hands of an Angry God" with the people's dramatic response, it's easy to say "that's what we need!" However, the real story of spiritual renewal begins years earlier in his home church as he preaches an extended doctrinal series on salvation (1735). It grasps the people's hearts and lives so they come to Christ, join the church, and experience true life in Christ.

As Pentecostalism enters its second century after the outpouring of the Spirit at Azusa Street, there appears to be a definite need for individuals, local churches and entire denominations to reexamine our basic doctrinal distinctive from both a Biblical and historical view. This stems from a great number of people not knowing why and what they believe about Spirit baptism and speaking in tongues.

Whether or not we want to recognize it, all of us can be influenced in our theology by dominant concepts within society. The "boomer generation" definitely highlights personal authority. Our emerging postmodern thought allows experience to reign. Plus, there is always the "third generation" demise which creeps in and takes over prior to many ever recognizing the plight.

This book stems from our desire for individuals and groups to study carefully the Scriptures, and then, in turn, experience the fullness of the Holy Spirit. When this occurs, congregations will be invigorated and enabled to be "salt and light" to the world (Matthew 5:13-15).

Part I
Prophetic Preparation

Empowered Leadership

What is at stake in the discussion of "initial evidence"? Does it really matter? What is the nature of "evidence"? Evidence of what? Is baptism in the Holy Spirit separate from regeneration or sanctification?

These and other questions must be addressed in this discussion. This work is not presented as an argument to convince a few, but as a plea to pursue truth and to pursue Holy Spirit fullness. This is not written merely as a doctrinal defense, but as a challenge to consecration, and as an encouragement to submission to God's plan and to receiving and affirming His provisions in your life.

Some basic truths must be reviewed in order to address the issue at hand. The person of the Holy Spirit will be noted, and then His ministry in the Old Testament will be discussed.

Even though the word *Spirit*, in both Hebrew and Greek, is sometimes translated "breath" or "wind," the Holy Spirit is not just a "Divine Influence," not just a "force." He is shown to be a Person, having abilities to think, to feel and to act (1 Corinthians 2:10-12; 12:11; Ephesians 4:30). He is a Divine Person, having the attributes of Deity, such as omnipotence (Luke 1:35) and omnipresence (Psalm 139:7-10). He is the *Holy* Spirit—"holy" describes His character. Several titles by which He is known are Another Comforter (or Helper), the Spirit of Truth, the Spirit of Life, and the Spirit of God (John 14:16, 17; Romans 8:2; 1 Corinthians 3:16).

The Holy Spirit was operative in the creative process of the earth. "The Spirit of God moved upon the face of the waters" (Genesis 1:2, KJV). From this indication of the Holy Spirit's involvement in shaping the cosmic mass in Genesis 1:2, all the way to the Holy Spirit's response of "Come" to Christ's announcement of His second advent in Revelation 22:17, we can see His vital activity throughout the Word of God.

OLD TESTAMENT EXAMPLES

In the Old Testament, the Holy Spirit strategically anointed individuals for leadership and frequently gave inspired utterances. Numbers 11 gives the account of Moses' frustration and desperation in bearing the burden of the complaining, murmuring and weeping Israelites. Moses cried to God for relief, and God answered with a plan of shared leadership. God instructed Moses to gather 70 of the elders of Israel and take them into the presence of God at the Tent of Meeting.

God said, "I will take of the Spirit that is upon you and will put the same upon them; and they shall bear the burden of the people with you, that you may not bear it yourself alone" (v. 17). When Moses had fulfilled the requests of the Lord, "the Lord came down in the cloud, and spoke to him, and took of the Spirit that was upon him, and placed the same upon the seventy elders; and it happened, when the Spirit rested upon them, that they prophesied, although they never did so again" (v. 25).

Prophesying, or "inspired utterances," indicated that the Spirit had come upon them to anoint them for the leadership tasks. This anointing was provided as a gift of the Sovereign Lord for the benefit of Moses and the rest of the people. This occasion indicated the necessity of the Spirit's wisdom and empowerment for the leadership of God's people. Charismatic personality, mere human wisdom, and acquired skills are not sufficient for spiritual leadership.

While the 70 elders were in the Tent of Meeting,
Eldad and Medad were still in the camp, and the
Spirit rested upon them. They began prophesying.
Again, prophesying is an indication of the Spirit's
resting upon them. Keil and Delitzsch said:

> "To prophesy" is to be understood gener-
> ally, and especially here, not as the fore-
> telling of future things, but as speaking in an
> ecstatic and elevated state of mind, under
> the impulse and inspiration of the Spirit of
> God, just like the "speaking in tongues,"
> which frequently followed the gift of the
> Holy Ghost in the days of the apostles. . . .
> This miraculous manifestation of the Spirit
> was intended simply to give to the whole
> nation the visible proof that God had
> endowed them with His Spirit, as helpers of
> Moses, and had given them the authority
> required for the experience of their calling.[1]

A messenger reported this incident to Moses.
Joshua, Moses' assistant, heard the report. Joshua
responded with "Moses my lord, forbid them! (v.
28). Moses said to Joshua, "Are you jealous for my
sake? Oh, that all the Lord's people were prophets
and that the Lord would put His Spirit upon
them!" (v. 29). What insight! Was this a prophetic
wish expressed? Moses wanted the Spirit to rest
not just on a few, but on *all* of the people of God.

The judges, or deliverers of Israel are also examples of the Holy Spirit's empowering certain individuals at appropriate times to accomplish specified tasks on behalf of the people of God. God himself chose the people upon whom He put His Spirit.

> When the children of Israel cried out to the Lord, the Lord raised up a deliverer for the children of Israel, who delivered them: Othniel, the son of Kenaz, Caleb's younger brother. The Spirit of the Lord came upon him, and he judged Israel. He went out to war, and the Lord delivered Cushan-Rishathaim king of Mesopotamia into his hand; and his hand prevailed over Cushan-Rishathaim (Judges 3:9, 10).

In a similar way, the Bible states, "The Spirit of the Lord came upon Gideon . . ." (6:34). "Then the Spirit of the Lord came upon Jephthah . . ." (11:29). On several occasions, it is stated, "the Spirit of the Lord moved mightily upon Samson" (14:6, 19; 15:14). These and others were directed and empowered by God to lead, to defend, and to deliver the people of Israel from their adversaries. Without the Spirit's help, Israel was victimized by the enemies.

Another group in the Old Testament upon whom the Spirit came was the kings of Israel. When the people of God demanded a king, God himself chose Saul and instructed Samuel to anoint him. Samuel announced to Saul some signs that would

verify God's anointing and appointment. Samuel
said Saul would meet a group of prophets and
"the Spirit of the Lord will come upon you, and
you will prophesy with them and be turned into
another man. And let it be, when these signs
come to you, that you do as the occasion
demands; for God is with you" (1 Samuel 10:6, 7).
Verse 9 continues: "So it was, when he had turned
his back to go from Samuel, that God gave him
another heart; and all those signs came to pass
that day." The "inspired utterances" confirmed to
Saul and to the people that God's anointing was
upon him. This anointing was preparing him for
his leadership position.

Later, when God rejected Saul, David was
anointed to be the king. "The Spirit of the Lord
came upon David from that day forward. . . .
But the Spirit of the Lord departed from Saul"
(16:13, 14).

*The prophets were anointed by the Holy Spirit to
reveal God's will to His people.* These individuals
were not self-appointed, but they were "called"
by God to be His spokespersons. God convinced
the prophets of their responsibility and ultimate
accountability (see Ezekiel 2; 3; 33). God encountered the prophets in many different ways. For
example, Ezekiel said:

"The heavens were opened and I saw visions of
God" (1:1).

"So the Spirit lifted me up and took me away" (3:14).

"Then the Spirit entered me and set me on my feet, and spoke with me" (v. 24).

"Then the Spirit of the Lord fell upon me, and said to me, 'Speak!' " (11:5).

The prophets revealed God's will through inspired utterances, parables, symbols and symbolic actions. They revealed God's truth with authority. If the majority of the people did not believe the message, the prophet spoke anyway. If the people rejected the message, ignored the message or refused to obey the message, the prophet spoke the truth anyway.

Many times the primary task of the prophets was to call the people of God back to Him. They warned God's people about following other gods and ignoring the true One. They warned about religious rituals that were not coupled with faith and right living. The prophets instructed the people about the requirements of righteousness (Micah 6:8). The prophets also encouraged God's people to change their behavior by offering them hope through His promises.

OLD TESTAMENT PROPHECIES

God's promises to His people were a part of the predictive element in prophetic utterances. Some of these promises had immediate fulfillment and others involved a more far-reaching fulfillment. God gave insight concerning the future activity of God among His people. He promised to His people a Redeemer, an anointed Deliverer, a Messiah-Prince. Speaking through Isaiah, the Lord said,

> There shall come forth a Rod from the stem of Jesse, and a Branch shall grow out of his roots. The Spirit of the Lord shall rest upon Him, the Spirit of wisdom and understanding, the Spirit of counsel and might, the Spirit of knowledge and of the fear of the Lord (Isaiah 11:1, 2).

Further describing the Messiah, Isaiah said prophetically,

> The Spirit of the Lord is upon Me, because the Lord has anointed Me to preach good tidings to the poor; He has sent Me to heal the brokenhearted, to proclaim liberty to the captives, and the opening of the prison to those who are bound (61:1, 2).

Ezekiel talks about the hope of Israel in God's future work.

> I will give you a new heart and put a new spirit within you; I will take the heart of stone out of your flesh and give you a heart

of flesh. I will put My Spirit within you and
cause you to walk in My statutes, and you
will keep My judgments and do them
(Ezekiel 36:26, 27).

The prophet Joel gives a far-reaching promise of
the outpouring of God's Spirit upon His people:

And it shall come to pass afterward that I
will pour out My Spirit on all flesh; your
sons and your daughters shall prophesy,
your old men shall dream dreams, your
young men shall see visions. And also on
My menservants and on My maidservants I
will pour out My Spirit in those days (Joel
2:28, 29).

The details of this prophecy will be discussed
later, but for now, please notice the word *afterward*.
To answer the question "After what?" the prior
events of Joel's prophecy must be considered. Joel
called on God's people to wake up and recognize
the terrible judgment of God on them. He encouraged them to lament and mourn, and to cry out to
God. Joel warned the people of the awesomeness
of the "Day of the Lord."
When the people realized their desolation and
desperation, the Lord spoke to them,

"'Now, therefore ... turn to Me with all your
heart, with fasting, with weeping, and with

mourning.' So rend your heart, and not your garments; return to the Lord your God, for He is gracious and merciful, slow to anger, and of great kindness; and He relents from doing harm" (2:12, 13).

God responded with His grace and steadfast love. He promised to remove their shame and reproach. He would drive away the army of locusts. He would bring back productivity to the land. He would restore those things that had been destroyed by the locusts. As the people enjoyed the blessings, their lament would be replaced with praise to the name of the Lord. They were assured that God would be in their midst. They would also know that the Lord was their God and that there was no other. At some unspecified time after this marvelous restoration, then, God would pour out His Spirit on those who are in right relationship to Him.

We have noted some examples of the activity of the Holy Spirit in Old Testament times, as well as some of the preparation for His future involvement. We are able to note these things because God chose to give us a record.

All Scripture is given by inspiration of God, and is profitable for doctrine, for reproof, for correction, for instruction in righteousness, that the man of God may be complete,

thoroughly equipped for every good work
(2 Timothy 3:16, 17).

Peter wrote:

Knowing this first, that no prophecy of
Scripture is of any private interpretation, for
prophecy never came by the will of man,
but holy men of God spoke as they were
moved by the Holy Spirit (2 Peter 1:20, 21).

The Holy Spirit enhanced the thinking of human
beings and directed them as they revealed to us
what God wanted us to know.

ENDNOTES

[1] C.F. Keil and F. Delitzsch, "The Pentateuch," *Biblical Commentary on the Old Testament*, trans. James Martin, vol. 3 (Grand Rapids: Eerdmans, 1991) 70, 71.

STUDY GUIDE
Lesson 1

Needed—Spirit-filled leaders! What are the basic qualifications of these leaders?

SCRIPTURES

"Oh, that all the Lord's people were prophets and that the Lord would put His Spirit upon them!" (Numbers 11:29).

"And it shall come to pass afterward that I will pour out My Spirit on all flesh; your sons and your daughters shall prophesy, your old men shall dream dreams, your young men shall see visions. And also on My menservants and on My maidservants I will pour out My Spirit in those days" (Joel 2:28, 29).

QUESTIONS AND READINGS

1. Read Numbers 11.

2. The word translated *Spirit* can also be translated how? *breath, wind*

3. What are the basic characteristics of "person"?
   think, feel, act

4. What indicates that the Holy Spirit is divine or deity? *'holy' character, omnipotent, omnipresent*

5. What are other titles by which the Holy Spirit is known? *Comporter, Spirit of Truth, Spirit of Life, Spirit of God.*

6. According to Numbers 11, how did God qualify the seventy to help Moses carry the leadership load? *He put on them the same Spirit on Moses — Holy Spirit.*

7. What was the evidence that the Spirit rested on these leaders? *Prophesy — inspired ecstatic utterances.*

8. Learn and quote the "prophetic wish" of Numbers 11:29.

9. How were the judges equipped to bring deliverance to Israel? *The 'Spirit of the Lord' moved upon them.*

10. Read 1 Samuel 10:1-26.

11. What confirmed to Saul and the people that God's anointing rested upon him? *He prophesied*

12. Note the different works of the Spirit indicated in Isaiah 11:1, 2; 61:1, 2; Ezekiel 36:26, 27; and Joel 2:28, 29.

13. Learn 2 Timothy 3:16, 17 and 2 Peter 1:20, 21.

APPLICATION

God sets the stage for spiritual leadership by showing the necessity of His Spirit's resting upon each leader. God also sets the pattern of "inspired utterances" as indicating the presence of the Holy Spirit to anoint for the leadership tasks. Please read Acts 6:1-7 and notice that being "full of the Holy Spirit" is a qualification of leaders in the early church.

God shows us His plans for the people of the "new covenant." He transforms their lives and, by the indwelling of His Holy Spirit, enables them to live godly lives. God shows His further plans to pour out His Spirit upon these in the "new covenant" that they all might proclaim the good news in spiritual power.

The Holy Spirit in the Life and Ministry of Jesus

The life and ministry of Jesus of Nazareth serve as fulfillment of many of the Old Testament prophecies. They also provide a pattern and further prophetic preparation for the fuller operation of the Holy Spirit in the people of God. In this section, we will trace the work of the Holy Spirit in the miraculous conception of Jesus; His reception in the Temple by Simeon; Jesus' wilderness temptation; His anointing for ministry and His resurrection. We will also consider some of Jesus' revelation to His disciples concerning the ministry of the Holy Spirit.

Among the Gospels, only Matthew and Luke record the birth narratives of Jesus. Matthew records the angel's announcement to Joseph that "the child conceived in her is from the Holy Spirit" (Matthew 1:20, *NRSV*). Luke gives us more details in the birth narrative he presents.

Responding to Mary's question about how could she have a baby since she was a virgin, the angel replied,

> "The Holy Spirit will come upon you, and the power of the Highest will overshadow you; therefore, also, that Holy One who is to be born will be called the Son of God" (Luke 1:35).

So in a mysterious and powerful way the Holy Spirit was involved in the conception of Jesus Christ. This baby was of divine origin.

The Holy Spirit was also involved in the reception of the child Jesus at the Temple. Simeon, the elderly priest, had been told by the Holy Spirit that he would not experience death until he had seen the Lord's Christ. On the day Joseph and Mary took Jesus to the Temple for dedication, the Holy Spirit prompted Simeon to go to the Temple (2:27). Simeon took the Christ child in his arms, prayed, blessed Mary and Joseph, and gave forth a prophecy concerning the child (see vv. 25-35).

So it was the Holy Spirit who revealed to Simeon the imminent arrival of the Messiah. The Holy Spirit directed Simeon so that he went to the Temple at the right time to participate in this great event.

All four Gospel accounts inform us of the role John the Baptist played as the "great introducer" (Matthew 3:1-12; Mark 1:2-8; Luke 3:1-20; John 1:6-8, 19-27). Powerfully, he prepared the way for the Messiah. He urged the people to repent and to be baptized in water. He insisted that lifestyle changes would result from genuine repentance. The preaching of John had such an impact that people started wondering if he were the Messiah. John quickly proclaimed, however,

> "I indeed baptize you with water; but One mightier than I is coming, whose sandal strap I am not worthy to loose. He will baptize you with the Holy Spirit and fire" (Luke 3:16).

The day John actually pointed out the Messiah, he declared,

> "Here is the Lamb of God who takes away the sin of the world! This is he of whom I said, 'After me comes a man who ranks ahead of me because he was before me.' I myself did not know him; but I came baptizing with water for this reason, that he might be revealed to Israel" (John 1:29-31, *NRSV*).

The Holy Spirit had anointed John to understand his prophetic place in the history of salvation. The Spirit had given him courage to withstand the public pressures to deviate from his appointment. John's preaching was pointed and powerful. Expectation and anticipation were revived in the people of God.

The baptism of Jesus by John in the Jordan River was a pivotal point in the ministry of John the Baptist. This scene could be viewed as divine anointing, confirmation and commendation. It could also be viewed as the inauguration of the public ministry of Jesus. When Jesus had been baptized, He was praying. While He was praying, the heavens opened and the Holy Spirit descended on Jesus in a bodily form like a dove (Luke 3:21, 22). John testified,

> "I saw the Spirit descending from heaven like a dove, and it remained on him. I myself did not know him, but the one who sent me to baptize with water said to me, 'He on whom you see the Spirit descend and remain is the one who baptizes with the Holy Spirit.' And I myself have seen and have testified that this is the Son of God" (John 1:32-34, *NRSV*).

The Spirit's descending in the form of a dove was visible evidence to John the Baptist that Jesus is the Spirit Baptizer, the very Son of God. The fact that the Holy Spirit remained on Jesus was the final convincing evidence for John.

Just as John immersed people in water, so Jesus immerses people in the Holy Spirit. The water was the element into which John immersed individuals; the Holy Spirit is the element into which Jesus immerses individuals. The heavens opened, the Holy Spirit descended, and a voice came from heaven, "You are My beloved Son; in You I am well pleased" (Luke 3:22).

God testified to the unique relationship between the Father and the Son. He also testified that the Son was well-pleasing to the Father. So the Father confirmed the person of Jesus and the character of Jesus. The Holy Spirit gave the ongoing anointing for the ministry of Jesus.

The Synoptic Gospels record that after the baptism of Jesus, the Holy Spirit directed Jesus into the wilderness of temptation. Matthew wrote,

> "Then Jesus was led up by the Spirit into the wilderness to be tempted by the devil" (Matthew 4:1).[1] Mark said, "Immediately the Spirit drove Him into the wilderness" (Mark 1:12).[2]

Being driven does not indicate resistance, but it shows the strong inner compulsion of the Holy Spirit. Luke gives us further details: "Jesus, being full of the Holy Spirit, returned from the Jordan and was led by the Spirit *into* the wilderness" (Luke 4:1, emphasis added).[3]

While Matthew and Mark tell us that the Spirit led Jesus *into* the wilderness, Luke reveals that the Spirit led Jesus while He was *in* the wilderness. Luke also indicates that Jesus was full of the Holy Spirit as He left the Jordan River and as He was being tempted in the wilderness. When the temptations ended and Satan departed, "Jesus returned in the power of the Spirit to Galilee" (Luke 4:14). So the Holy Spirit abode in, directed and empowered Jesus.

Jesus went to His hometown of Nazareth, and in the synagogue He read from the scroll of Isaiah. The passage in Isaiah 61:1, 2 is the model of Jesus' earthly ministry:

> The Spirit of the Lord is upon Me, because He has anointed Me to preach the gospel to the poor; He has sent Me to heal the broken-hearted, to proclaim liberty to the captives and recovery of sight to the blind, to set at liberty those who are oppressed; to proclaim the acceptable year of the Lord (Luke 4:18, 19).

Part of Jesus' sermon was, "Today this Scripture is fulfilled in your hearing" (v. 21). Jesus accepted this prophetic utterance to be the model, outline and direction for His ministry. He affirmed the reality of the Holy Spirit's pressing in on Him and anointing Him for the fulfillment of His mission. The presence and power of the Holy Spirit characterized the ministry of Jesus.

Simon Peter recognized the role of the Holy Spirit in the life and ministry of Jesus. He said, "How God anointed Jesus of Nazareth with the Holy Spirit and with power, who went about doing good and healing all who were oppressed by the devil, for God was with Him" (Acts 10:38). At the outset of His ministry, Jesus confirmed the leading, empowering and anointing of the Holy Spirit to bring freedom. After Jesus' earthly ministry, Peter confirmed the continued anointing and empowerment of the Holy Spirit in the life of Jesus as He completed His mission of healing, delivering and setting people free.

ENDNOTES

[1] Matthew uses the word *anag_* (was led up).

[2] Mark uses the word *ekball_* (thrusts forth). Same word is used for "casting out" in relationship to demons.

[3] Luke uses the word *ag_* (was led) and *en* (in) the wilderness, while Matthew and Mark use *eis* (into) the wilderness.

STUDY GUIDE
Lesson 2

If Jesus depended upon the Holy Spirit in order to accomplish His mission, how much more should we depend upon the Holy Spirit in order to accomplish our mission!

SCRIPTURE

"How God anointed Jesus of Nazareth with the Holy Spirit and with power, who went about doing good and healing all who were oppressed by the devil, for God was with Him" (Acts 10:38).

QUESTIONS AND READINGS

Read Matthew 1—4 and Luke 1—4.

From this listing, choose the correct answers to the statements below.

a. The Synoptic Gospels
b. Spirit's descending like a dove
c. Holy Spirit
d. Matthew
e. Simeon
f. Mark
g. Isaiah 61
h. Luke
i. Water
j. John

_____ 1. These two writers record that the Holy Spirit was involved in the conception of Jesus Christ.

_____ 2. This man was led by the Spirit to the reception of Jesus at the Temple.

_____ 3. These writers inform us of the role John the Baptist fulfilled as the "Great Introducer."

_____ 4. This event gave visible evidence to John the Baptist that Jesus is the Spirit Baptizer, the very Son of God.

_____ 5. The element into which John immersed individuals

_____ 6. The element into which Jesus immerses individuals

_____ 7. These record that the Holy Spirit directed Jesus into the wilderness of temptation.

_____ 8. This passage records the model of Jesus' earthly ministry.

APPLICATION

The presence of the Holy Spirit characterized the entire life and ministry of Jesus. The Holy Spirit led, anointed and empowered Jesus to fulfill His mission.

If we, indeed, are going to continue the ministry of Jesus Christ, we desperately need the Holy Spirit to lead us, to anoint us and to empower us.

Jesus' Prophetic Preparation for His Disciples

Full of the Holy Spirit, Jesus was powerfully equipped for fulfilling His mission. As He neared the time of the Crucifixion, Jesus became more urgent in preparing His disciples to be receptive to the fullness of the Holy Spirit. He knew they would desperately need the leading, anointing, instructing and empowering of the Holy Spirit to carry out their mission.

While He was on the earth, Jesus fully directed His disciples. He instructed them, corrected them, rebuked them, encouraged them, cleansed them, and authorized them to work the works of God. They fully depended on Him. When they did not understand His public teaching, He further enlightened them (Matthew 13:36-43). When they were powerless to cast out a demon, He intervened and expelled the demon (17:16-18). When the disciples rejoiced that demons were subject to them, Jesus redirected their rejoicing: "Do not rejoice in this, that the spirits are subject to you, but rather rejoice because your names are written in heaven" (Luke 10:20). Jesus was their Teacher, Helper, Counselor, Strengthener and Advocate.

Jesus tried to prepare His disciples for His departure and the importance of their receiving "Another Strengthener" (see John 14:16). *Another* means "similar to but distinct from."[1] This One would be similar to Jesus. The word translated *Counselor, Comforter, Helper, Strengthener, Advocate, Interceder* or *Paraclete* means "one called to the side of for the purpose of helping."[2] Some translations use the word *Comforter* because it is derived from two words meaning "with" and "strong."[3] So this "Coming One" would supply them with strength and power. Some of His other ministries would be teaching, guiding, instructing and enlightening (John 14:25, 26; 16:12, 13).

The coming of "Another Strengthener" is dependent on the completion of Jesus Christ's redemptive activity. Divine incarnation, a perfect life, sacrificial death, resurrection and ascension are necessary.

Again, this involved laying aside the outward manifestations of glory, drawing on the power of the Holy Spirit to accomplish His mission, giving Himself for our sins in crucifixion, being raised from the dead to confirm His victories, and experiencing the complete restoration of glory at the right hand of the Father.

Jesus informed His disciples, "But now I go away to Him who sent Me, and none of you asks Me, 'Where are You going?' But because I have said these things to you, sorrow has filled your heart. Nevertheless I tell you the truth. It is to your advantage that I go away; for if I do not go away, the Helper will not come to you; but if I depart, I will send Him to you" (16:5-7). Jesus' departure was necessary for their receiving the fulfillment of His promise. His departure involved crucifixion, resurrection and ascension.

Earlier, Jesus had talked of a future time when believers would have such a bountiful supply of spiritual provisions that a life-giving flow would come from their inner being (7:38). John said,

> "But this He spoke concerning the Spirit,
> whom those believing in Him would receive;
> for the Holy Spirit was not yet given, because
> Jesus was not yet glorified" (v. 39).

Jesus further encouraged His disciples with the promise,

> "Most assuredly, I say to you, he who
> believes in Me, the works that I do he will do
> also; and greater works than these he will do,
> because I go to My Father" (14:12).

The continuation of the ministry of Jesus in the lives of believers depended on Jesus' glorification and the subsequent Holy Spirit fullness in answer to His request.

Holy Spirit fullness is a gift of the Father and the Son. Jesus told His disciples, "If you love Me, keep My commandments, and I will pray the Father, and He will give you another Helper, that He may abide with you forever" (vv. 15, 16). The word translated *pray* means "to request something from one who is your equal."[4] Jesus gave the request, and the Father gave the Spirit. The Father sends the Holy Spirit in the name of Jesus (v. 26). Jesus also told His disciples, "I will send Him to you from the Father" (see 15:26; 16:7).

There is no contradiction because the Father and the Son mutually sent the Holy Spirit. Simon Peter shared the truths of Jesus' crucifixion and resurrection, then said,

> "Therefore being exalted to the right hand of
> God, and having received from the Father
> the promise of the Holy Spirit, He poured out
> this which you now see and hear" (Acts 2:33).

So Simon seemed to understand the close connection of crucifixion, resurrection, ascension and
Spirit fullness.

On the day Jesus arose from the dead, He
appeared to His disciples and said, "'Peace be
with you.' When He had said this, He showed
them His hands and His side. Then the disciples
were glad when they saw the Lord. So Jesus said
to them again, 'Peace to you! As the Father has
sent Me, I also send you.' And when He had said
this, He breathed on them, and said to them,
'Receive the Holy Spirit'" (John 20:19-22). The disciples were afraid and confused. Jesus' words,
"Peace to you," were more than a casual greeting,
a mere "Hello." These words were giving the
peace He had promised (14:27; 16:33).

The scars in His hands and side assured them
that this resurrected One before them was the
same One they had seen crucified. The sadness,
turmoil and fear were replaced with rejoicing at
the presence and proclamation of the risen Lord.
Jesus then connected the commissioning with the
pronouncement of peace, and He connects the
reception of the Holy Spirit to the commissioning.
Dr. R.H. Gause's insight on this teaching is excep-
tionally helpful:

> His first words "Peace to you" (20:19), are
> words of atonement. . . . Christ here

> announces peace with God. This is the peace
> of God's reconciliation in justification and
> regeneration. . . . There is a fundamental con-
> nection between the peace which Christ
> announced and the commission which He
> gave. It is a redemptive union. . . . Following
> this commission, our Lord "breathed on
> them" and He says to them, "Receive the Holy
> Spirit" (v. 22). His breathing is a symbol of His
> bestowal of the gift of the Holy Spirit from His
> divine person. His words are the command of
> receptivity.[5] In Jesus' words are both a promise
> and a command to be receptive.[6]

Just before ascending into heaven, Jesus gave the
promise, the instruction and the command to His
disciples concerning the coming of the Holy Spirit.
He talked again about the necessity of His crucifixion, the certainty of His resurrection, the urgency of
proclaiming repentance and forgiveness of sins, and
the imperative of divine power. "Behold, I send the
Promise of My Father upon you; but tarry in the city
of Jerusalem until you are endued with power from
on high" (Luke 24:49).

We noted earlier that Joel 2:28-32 was one of
those times the promise of the outpouring of the
Holy Spirit was given by the Father. The Promise of
the Father is the promise of power. Although fulfilling the Great Commission is urgent, it is imperative

for believers to be "clothed upon" with power from on high, in order to fulfill the Commission. Jesus instructed them—actually commanded them—to wait until they had received this power. The "Promise of the Father," "being clothed with power," and "baptized in the Holy Spirit" are used synonymously. This baptism in the Holy Spirit would occur before many days expired (Acts 1:5). As surely as John baptized believers in water, just that surely Jesus would baptize believers in the Holy Spirit.

Jesus reiterated this promise of power to His disciples: "But you shall receive power when the Holy Spirit has come upon you; and you shall be witnesses to Me in Jerusalem, and in all Judea and Samaria, and to the end of the earth" (v. 8). Jesus promised power so they could fulfill the mission to which He had called them. "The promise of power as a manifestation of the Spirit assures the disciples that Jesus will not abandon them to their own resources. Rather, they will be fully equipped for their task as witnesses. Indeed, they will receive the same power with which Jesus executed His earthly ministry. Therefore, just as the mission of Jesus had been inaugurated in the power of the Spirit, so at Pentecost the mission of the disciples was inaugurated in the power of the Spirit."[7]

ENDNOTES

[1] Leon Morris, *The Gospel According to John: The New International Commentary on the New Testament* (Grand Rapids: Eerdmans, 1971) 662. *Allos* is said to mean "another of the same kind."

[2] William F. Arndt and F. Wilbur Gingrich, *A Greek-English Lexicon of the New Testament* (U of Chicago P, 1957) 642. It is only the Holy Spirit that is expressly called παρακλητος *(or Paraclete)* in the Fourth Gospel.

[3] Morris, 664. Latin *con* and *fortis*.

[4] M.R. Vincent, *Word Studies in the New Testament* (Wilmington, DE: Associated Publishers and Authors, 1972) 466. "*Erotao* is to ask on equal terms, and hence is always used by Christ of His own asking from the Father, in the consciousness of His equal dignity."

[5] R. Hollis Gause, *Living in the Spirit: The Way of Salvation* (Cleveland, TN: Pathway, 1980) 66.

[6] Herschel Hobbs, *An Exposition of the Gospel of John* (Grand Rapids: Baker, 1968) 285. Hobbs said that "*receive* is in the ingressive aorist tense. So it could mean 'Begin to receive ye the Holy Spirit.' In view of His commission they were to begin even then to prepare themselves for the Holy Spirit's power when He should come at Pentecost."

Leon Morris, 289. Morris said, "This is promissory and anticipatory to the actual coming of the Spirit at Pentecost."

Howard M. Ervin, *Spirit Baptism* (Peabody, MA: Hendrickson, 1987) 17. Ervin argues that the aorist imperative *labete* (receive) must be point action. He believed that they actually received "new, spiritual life—they were born again—by the breath of God, the Son." This was still viewed as preparatory for and not identical with the Pentecostal outpouring.

[7] Roger Stronstad, *The Charismatic Theology of St. Luke* (Peabody, MA: Hendrickson, 1984) 52.

STUDY GUIDE
Lesson 3

Knowing that the very survival of His disciples depended on Him, Jesus had to encourage them by sharing the plan and provisions of the triune God on their behalf. He knew they would face questions, confusions, hostilities and overwhelming challenges. Jesus assured His disciples that He and the Father would send "Another Strengthener," the Holy Spirit, who would lead, anoint, instruct and empower them to fulfill their mission.

SCRIPTURE

"And I will pray the Father, and He will give you another Helper, that He may abide with you forever" (John 14:16).

QUESTIONS AND READINGS

Read John 14—16.
Fill in the blanks:

1. The word _____ means "similar to, but distinct from."

2. The word _____ means "one called alongside to help."

3. When Jesus said, "I will pray the Father," the

word translated *pray* means to make a request from someone who is your _____.

4. The "promise of the Father," "being clothed with power," and "_____" are used synonymously.

5. The word *Comforter* can also be translated as

   _____, _____,

   _____, _____

   or _____.

6. The Holy Spirit would provide teaching, guiding, instructing, enlightening and _____ for the disciples.

7. The completion of Jesus' redemptive activity involved Divine Incarnation, a perfect life, _____, the Resurrection and Ascension.

8. Jesus' departure, necessary for the fullness of the Spirit for the disciples, involved the Crucifixion, Resurrection and _____.

9. In John 20:19-22, "Peace to you" (words of atonement), "I send you" (words of commissioning) and "_____" (provision of power) are connected.

10. In John 20:22, "Receive the Holy Spirit" is a _____ and a command to be receptive.

APPLICATION

As Jesus' ministry was carried out in the power of the Holy Spirit, He knew the disciples' ministry must also be in the power of the Holy Spirit. Jesus informed them and instructed them concerning divine provision and commanded them to be receptive to Holy Spirit fullness.

Part II
Biblical Fulfillment

Baptism in the Holy Spirit

CONVICTION, REGENERATION, SANCTIFICATION

The Holy Spirit is at work in every believer. Before the person made a commitment to Jesus Christ, it was the Holy Spirit who brought the conviction of a need. The Holy Spirit convinced the person of the reality, heinousness and pervasiveness of sin. Sin is a controlling power from which only God can deliver. The Holy Spirit convinced the individual of the person and provisions of Jesus Christ. The Holy Spirit convinced the individual of judgment and accountability before God (John 16:8).

Sin is not just a nuisance; it is a power that separates us from God and righteousness. Without God, sin leads to eternal destruction. When a person sincerely repents and turns fully to Jesus Christ

59

in faith, the Holy Spirit conveys the atoning provisions of Christ to the person's life. The Holy Spirit brings new spiritual life to a person through regeneration. This "new birth," or "birth from above," is a necessary work of divine grace. It rescues a person from darkness and death and brings light and life. In regeneration, the seed of righteousness is implanted so that righteous fruit can be produced. Jesus told Nicodemus that no one can see nor enter into the kingdom of heaven without being born of the Spirit (John 3).

Understanding and entering into God's kingdom are not dependent on intellectual apprehension, religious ritual, religious affirmation or religious sacrifices; but on a supernatural work of the Holy Spirit. The repentant sinner is declared righteous in the sight of God, and the Holy Spirit enters the person and imparts the righteousness of Christ. The individual is birthed into the family of God by the Holy Spirit and incorporated into the body of Christ by the Holy Spirit (Titus 3:5; 1 Corinthians 12:12, 13; Romans 8:9).

The person receives the Spirit of Adoption who affirms all the legal rights of being a child of God and brings a freedom of responsiveness whereby the child can affectionately say, "Father." The Holy Spirit brings a unique connection between the Holy Spirit and the human spirit and He testifies to and confirms this newfound relationship of being truly a child of God (Romans 8:15, 16). *To become a child of God is to receive the Holy Spirit and to be blessed by His working.*

As regeneration is a work of the Holy Spirit, so sanctification is a work of the Holy Spirit in the life of a believer. Sanctification comes as a result of Christ's prayer, His atonement provision, the Word of God and the work of the Holy Spirit. John 17 records a prayer Jesus prayed for the sanctification of His disciples. The scope of that prayer is more far-reaching than we can include in this limited discussion, but let's note some of the essentials.

The disciples for whom Jesus prayed were given to Christ by the Father, granted eternal life, and taken out of the world system. They accepted God's Word and were obedient to it. They were convinced that Jesus was from the Father and sent by the Father. They were hated by the world system, but were given glory by Jesus Christ. Jesus said that in this prayer He was not praying for the world (unbelievers), but for those who belonged to God. These disciples were already separated unto God, separated unto Christ, and separated from the world system. They were still on the earth but not part of the evil system of values, pursuits and lifestyles. He did not request their consecration at this point, but He requested a work of divine grace.

The scope of Jesus' prayer was broadened so as to include all who would believe in Him through the disciples' message. Jesus' prayer includes us. In answer to His prayer, the believers are purified. Believers experience a full measure of Christ's joy and love. Believers are kept from the Evil One, even though they are sent into his domain of evil. Believers experience genuine unity—a unity that testifies to unbelievers that the Father has sent Jesus and that divine love flows from Him (John 17).

The answer to this prayer is guaranteed by Jesus' coming from the Father, completing His mission, and returning to the Father and the rightful glory of His Being. The believer not only experiences the answer to Jesus' prayer here and now, but anticipates the answer to His concluding request, "Father, I desire that those You have given Me may be with Me where I am, in order that they may keep on beholding My glory which You have given to Me because You loved Me before the foundation of the world" (v. 24, my translation).

As Jesus ascended to the Father and the restoration of His glory, the disciples exhibited some of the answers to Jesus' prayer. The disciples returned to Jerusalem with great joy and were continually in the Temple blessing God (Luke 24:52, 53). Before, when Jesus even mentioned going away, sorrow gripped their hearts, but now He actually went away and they were filled with joy.

The disciples returned to Jerusalem in full obedience to Christ's command to wait in Jerusalem until they received the Promise of the Father. The unity that characterized their waiting in worship was evidence of a divine operation. "These all continued with one accord in prayer" (Acts 1:14). In sanctification, the Holy Spirit purges the individual of all that hinders the full operation of divine love.

The Holy Spirit moves the believer to receive and live in all the provisions of divine grace. None of these blessings are earned or deserved; but they are anticipated, asked for and received by faith in the Promiser. God provides power for the believer to live a holy life, to worship God acceptably and to witness effectively.

DISTINCT EXPERIENCE

If the Holy Spirit is at work in every believer, does that mean that every believer is baptized in the Holy Spirit? If every believer is indwelt by the Spirit, does that mean every believer is baptized in the Holy Spirit? Is baptism in the Holy Spirit separate from regeneration and sanctification? Is baptism in the Holy Spirit for sinners or believers? We need to find Biblical answers to these questions.

We, the authors, have a high view of Scriptural authority. We believe the Holy Spirit anointed, inspired and guided the human writers. We take into account the personality, training and vocabulary of the human writers. The historical and spiritual contexts are considered. The purposes, themes and major emphases of each writer are also considered. These various considerations do not detract from our belief in divine inspiration, but certainly help us in interpretation.

The form of literature has to be considered. Whether it is literal or figurative language has to be assessed. Word usage should also be studied. This involves the meaning of the root word, how it is generally used; its usage in the Old Testament; its usage in the Septuagint; its usage in the New Testament; how it is usually used by this individual writer and how the word is used in this context.

This process may seem complicated, but it is important. One cannot look in a concordance, find a word used in several locations, and assume that the word means the same thing in each place. If we follow basic principles of interpretation, we will not view the theology of the Holy Spirit in John, Paul and Luke as contradictory, but as complementary.

We have noted already in John's Gospel such things as regeneration, sanctification, promises of Another Strengthener, the bestowal of peace, the commissioning of the disciples, and the command to receive the Holy Spirit. We have noted briefly some of Paul's statements concerning the operation of the Holy Spirit, and we will look at more.

At this point, however, let's consider some of Luke's writings. There is widespread agreement that Luke, the beloved physician and traveling companion of Paul, wrote the two-volume Luke and Acts. Luke addressed these two books to Theophilus. The name means "lover of God" or "friend of God." The books, therefore, could be addressed to each lover of God, even though it was likely a fellow Christian or "God-fearer."[1]

In the Gospel, Luke said he had investigated everything carefully or accurately from the beginning, and was writing an orderly account so that Theophilus could know the reliability of the things about which he had been instructed (Luke 1:3, 4). Luke's preface to the Book of Acts says:

> The former account I made, O Theophilus, of all that Jesus began both to do and teach, until the day in which He was taken up, after He through the Holy Spirit had given commandments to the apostles whom He had chosen. . . . And being assembled together with them, He commanded them not to depart from Jerusalem, but to wait for the Promise of the Father, "which," He said, "you have heard from Me; for John truly baptized with water, but you shall be baptized with the Holy Spirit not many days from now. . . . But you shall receive power when the Holy Spirit has come upon you; and you shall be witnesses to Me in Jerusalem, and in

all Judea and Samaria, and to the end of the
earth" (Acts 1:1, 2, 4, 5, 8).

These introductory statements set the tone of
the Book of Acts. The book shows how the Holy
Spirit continued the ministry of Jesus through the
disciples.

The preface of Acts restates the conclusion of
Luke's Gospel and continues the story. As a physician, Luke had been accustomed to giving attention
to detail. In addition to his own skills and propensi-
ties, the Holy Spirit heightened his sensitivity and
guided his research. The Holy Spirit guided his
selection and arrangement of the materials in his
accounts. Details are carefully chosen and presented
so that the message will be received. Luke was both
a first-rate historian and a theologian. Luke provides us with narrative theology. Stronstad said:

> [Luke's] episodes are historical-theological in
> intent. In other words, Luke never intended
> to give his readers a simple description of
> events, either to inform or to satisfy the
> curiosity of his readers about the origins of
> their faith. Therefore, however the details are
> worked out, in principle, Luke's narratives
> are an important and legitimate database for
> constructing a Lucan doctrine of the Spirit.
> Thus, rather than providing a flimsy founda-
> tion upon which to erect a doctrine of the

Holy Spirit, as is commonly alleged, the historical accounts of the activity of the Spirit in Acts provide a firm foundation for erecting a doctrine of the Spirit which has normative implications for the mission and religious experience of the contemporary church."[2]

Luke uses several terms for being baptized in the Holy Spirit: "baptized with the Holy Spirit" (Luke 3:16; Acts 1:5; 11:16); "filled with the Holy Spirit" (Acts 2:4; 9:17); "receive the Holy Spirit" (2:38; 8:15; 10:47; 19:2); "come upon" (1:8); "fall upon" (8:16; 10:44; 11:15); "endued [clothed] with power" (Luke 24:49); "poured out" (Acts 2:17, 18; 10:45); "promise" (Luke 24:49; Acts 2:39); and "gift" (Acts 2:38; 10:45; 11:17). These terms are used interchangeably in reference to the same experience—being baptized in the Holy Spirit. Not one of these expressions nor all of them together can capture the full meaning of this experience. These are metaphorical terms used by Luke as he tries to describe these marvelous occurrences.

Human language is strained when seeking to communicate this divine-human encounter. We are filled with a sense of awe, wonder and majesty as we consider God's workings. To seek to put into words an experience with God is a humbling experience. We do our best to articulate the experience, but ultimately we urge each person to experience that which is inexpressible. Because we are incapable of adequately expressing the experience should not hinder us from experiencing what God has provided for us, however.

Luke consistently connects being baptized in the Holy Spirit with being equipped with divine power to fulfill a divine mission. In his Gospel, the emphasis is on the Holy Spirit's empowering Jesus for His mission. Navone calls Luke's Gospel "The Gospel of the Spirit," and says that Luke emphasizes the role of the Holy Spirit more than the other Gospels.[3] In Acts, Luke shows the intricate connection between being baptized in the Holy Spirit and the power demonstrated in proclaiming the gospel of Jesus Christ.

> "Therefore, since the gift of the Spirit to Jesus inaugurates and empowers His mission, then, whatever meaning Spirit baptism might have in other contexts, it has the same primary meaning for the mission of the disciples as the anointing by the Spirit had for the charismatic mission of Jesus."[4]

When Jesus urged His disciples to await the Promise of the Father, He said they would be clothed upon with power from on high. He did not talk of forgiveness of sins. He did not speak of the beginning of the body of Christ, or the church. Jesus promised them power for the fulfillment of

their mission. Jesus promised that this power
would be received when they were baptized in
the Holy Spirit.

It is evident that the people baptized in the Holy
Spirit on the Day of Pentecost were disciples of
Jesus. They were committed to, and obedient to,
Jesus. What about the Samaritans? Scripture says,

> The multitudes with one accord heeded the
> things spoken by Philip . . . and there was
> great joy in that city. . . . When they believed
> Philip as he preached the things concerning
> the kingdom of God and the name of Jesus
> Christ, both men and women were baptized.
> . . . Samaria had received the word of God
> (Acts 8:6, 8, 12, 14).

These believers had listened, received, believed,
obeyed, were baptized in water, and later received
the Holy Spirit baptism.

Acts 9 tells the story of Saul. After being struck
down on the road to Damascus and after the Lord
identified Himself as Jesus, the One whom Saul
was persecuting, Saul's response was, "Lord, what
do You want me to do?" (v. 6). Saul obeyed the
instructions given to him and went into the city to
await further word. The Lord told Ananias that
Saul was praying and he was "a chosen vessel of
Mine to bear My name before Gentiles, kings, and

the children of Israel" (vv. 11, 15). Ananias laid his hands on Saul and said, "Brother Saul, the Lord Jesus, who appeared to you on the road as you came, has sent me that you may receive your sight and be filled with the Holy Spirit" (v. 17). Three days passed between his commitment to Jesus as Lord and his receiving the Holy Spirit.

Cornelius was a devout and generous man who always prayed to God. He was one whose prayers and generosity in giving had become a memorial before God (10:4). An angel communicated a message to Cornelius and he obeyed. Jesus said to Peter, "What God has cleansed you must not call common" (v. 15). Part of Peter's sermon was, "The word which God sent to the children of Israel, preaching peace through Jesus Christ—He is Lord of all—that word you know, which was proclaimed throughout all Judea, and began from Galilee after the baptism which John preached" (vv. 36, 37).

"The words *you know* seem to indicate that not only were these God-fearing Gentiles acquainted with the ministry of Jesus, but they were already converted. . . . They were already saved, for before Peter arrived in Caesarea, God had granted to them repentance that leads to life." [5] "A strong case can be made that Cornelius and company were already members of the people of God as defined by Luke." [6]

The believers baptized in the Spirit at Ephesus, according to Acts 19, were called *disciples*. Dr. French Arrington said: *"Disciples* in the writings of Luke always means Christians. The disciples that Paul met at Ephesus were not half-believers or merely disciples of John the Baptist, but Christian believers. . . . The twelve at Ephesus were Christians of a pre-Pentecostal kind. They had been converted but not filled with the Spirit."[7]

Paul asked a question that can be translated two ways, depending on the context. The first way is, "Did you receive the Holy Spirit when you believed?" (Acts 19:2). The context here indicates the better choice is, "Did you receive the Holy Spirit *after* you believed?"

Paul accepted them and addressed them as "believers." He knew that as believers they had the Spirit, but the question has to do with the Charismatic outpouring, or being baptized in the Spirit. These believers had limited knowledge. They had been baptized by John, who preached Christ, and on further instruction were baptized in the name of the Lord Jesus. They did not know that the baptism in the Holy Spirit that John had predicted had actually been fulfilled.

The very question that Paul asked them indicated his concern that every believer be baptized in the Holy Spirit. It seemed to be an urgent matter to him.

The accounts in the Book of Acts show us Luke's intention, as he is directed by the Spirit, to connect the baptizing in the Holy Spirit with Charismatic power for mission and not with salvation. The gift of the Holy Spirit "goes beyond salvation; it is promised to those who repent and come to faith in Jesus Christ."[8]

ENDNOTES

[1] John Nolland, *Word Biblical Commentary Luke 1-9-20*, vol. 35A (Dallas: Word, 1989) XXXIII.

[2] Roger Stronstad, *The Charismatic Theology of St. Luke* (Peabody, MA: Hendrickson, 1984) 9.

[3] John J. Navone, *Themes of St. Luke* (Rome: Gregorian, 1970).

[4] Stronstad, 52.

[5] French Arrington, *The Acts of the Apostles* (Peabody, MA: Hendrickson, 1988) 112, 113.

[6] Donald A. Johns, "Some New Directions in the Hermeneutics of Classical Pentecostalism's Doctrine of Initial Evidence," in *Initial Evidence*, Gary B. McGee, ed. (Peabody, MA: Hendrickson, 1991) 151.

[7] Arrington, 191.

[8] William J. Rodman, *Renewal Theology*, vol. 2 (Grand Rapids: Zondervan, 1990) 205, 206. Note further here his quotations (205): "William Neil rightly sees the gift of the Spirit as the gift of the new power which Peter's audience has seen at work in the Pentecostal experience of the Apostles and their associates" (*The Acts of the Apostles*, NCBC, 79). Neil does not connect this gift with salvation. Eduard Schweizer writes that in Acts "salvation is never ascribed to the Spirit. According to Acts 2:38 the Spirit is imparted to those who are already converted and baptised" (TDNT, 6:412). Hermann

Gunkel similarly declares, "For Acts it is a common-place that to be a believer and to be seized by the Spirit are separate events" (*The Influence of the Holy Spirit*, 17). Kirsopp Lake states that in the various Acts passages that deal with the gift of the Spirit "there is no suggestion of regeneration by the Spirit, or of the view that salvation depends on it" (*The Acts of the Apostles*, 5:109). Nor does Calvin, it is interesting to observe, attach salvation to the early gift of the Spirit (*The Acts of the Apostles*, 1:120). He writes concerning Acts 2:38: "Remission of sins and newness of life were the principal things, and this [the gift of the Holy Spirit] was, as it were, *an addition* [italics mine]." The "addition," according to Calvin, was "that Christ should show forth unto them his power by some visible gift."

STUDY GUIDE
Lesson 4

Is every believer indwelt by the Holy Spirit? Is every believer baptized in the Holy Spirit?

Is baptism in the Holy Spirit separate from regeneration?

SCRIPTURES

"Behold, I send the Promise of My Father upon you; but tarry in the city of Jerusalem until you are endued with power from on high" (Luke 24:49).

"But you shall receive power when the Holy Spirit has come upon you; and you shall be witnesses to Me in Jerusalem, and in all Judea and Samaria, and to the end of the earth" (Acts 1:8).

QUESTIONS AND READINGS

1. What is the work of the Holy Spirit in the life of an unbeliever? (Note John 16:8-11.)

2. What happens in regeneration or the new birth?

3. Read John 17 and list the characteristics of the people for whom Jesus was praying. Are these believers or unbelievers?

4. From John 17, discuss the results of sanctification and how these appear in the lives of disciples prior to Holy Spirit baptism.

5. Note carefully the connections between Luke's

Gospel and the Book of Acts, especially the emphasis on the Holy Spirit in each.

6. Why are Luke's writings called "narrative theology"?

7. List several different terms that are used interchangeably with "baptized in the Holy Spirit."

8. How do the Scriptures indicate that Cornelius and family were already part of the people of God?

9. What evidence is there to show that the disciples at Ephesus were already Christians?

10. Discuss Luke's intention to connect the baptizing in the Holy Spirit with charismatic power for mission rather than with salvation.

APPLICATION

As Christian believers, we celebrate life in Jesus Christ and the indwelling of the Holy Spirit. We appreciate the Holy Spirit's having convicted us of our sin, regenerating us, adopting us into the family of God, and confirming in our hearts that we really are the children of God. We appreciate the sanctifying work the Holy Spirit is doing within us. Shouldn't we also desire intently that Jesus baptize us in the Holy Spirit so that we might be equipped with divine power to fulfill the divine mission?

Speaking in Tongues

The disciples who chose to obey Jesus' command to wait in Jerusalem were gathered in the Upper Room. They were filled with joy. They were filled with love, and this gave them unity or "togetherness." Together they worshiped, prayed, praised and extolled God. They were together in obedience. They were together in expectation of Jesus' fulfilling His Promise. Jesus had told them it would not be many days, but they did not know how long.

Acts 2

In His sovereignty, God chose to grant the outpouring of the Holy Spirit on the Day of Pentecost. The Feast of Pentecost was a joyous celebration of God's faithfulness in giving an abundant harvest. While the Feast of Passover meant sacrifice and

77

suffering, the Feast of Pentecost meant abundance and joy. "In later Judaism it was believed to be the anniversary of the giving of the Law at Sinai."[1]

Suddenly, there came a sound from heaven as a rushing, mighty wind and tongues as of fire appeared. Both of these sights and sounds would remind these participants of an Old Testament theophany recorded in Exodus 19:16-20. In the Exodus account, after the sights and sounds, God spoke.

In the Upper Room, these sights and sounds assured them that what followed was from God. "And they were all filled with the Holy Spirit and began to speak with other tongues, as the Spirit gave them utterance" (Acts 2:4). The sound from heaven filled the room where they were sitting. The gift from heaven filled their being. It did not originate from within but from above. The promise of John the Baptist—"He will baptize you in the Holy Spirit" (Luke 3:16)—was being fulfilled. They were filled, immersed in, saturated in, and clothed upon with power from on high.

Again, all attempts at describing this encounter are inadequate. When the disciples were filled, they began to speak in a totally different language from their native tongue, as the Spirit "kept giving them the language and the appropriate words."[2] "In Old Testament times the regular consequences of a man's being possessed by the Spirit of God was that he prophesied. So it was with Eldad and

Medad when the Spirit rested upon them in the camp of Israel (Numbers 11:26ff.), and so it was with many others. So now the descent of the Holy Spirit on the disciples was manifested by prophetic speech, but prophetic speech of a peculiar kind. They "began to speak with other tongues as the Spirit gave them utterance."[3]

These 120 individuals had been praising God in their own language as they worshiped. Now fully immersed in the Holy Spirit, they freely spoke what the Spirit was giving, which was exalted praises to the mighty acts of God. Although they were filled with the Spirit, the Holy Spirit did not commandeer their being and speak through them. Rather, the Spirit prompted and directed them, and they spoke. This signifies full submission to God and complete trust in Him.

Some of these were speaking known languages, because many who were in Jerusalem for the Feast of Pentecost heard them speaking in their own dialects. Many of the listeners were devout individuals, and they were amazed as they heard and understood these Galileans speak forth the mighty works of God. Curious, they were asking one another, "What does this mean?" Others had a totally different response. They said, "They are filled with new wine" (Acts 2:12, 13, *NRSV*). We do not know what aroused this skepticism and hostility. Perhaps some heard speech that was not a known language. Perhaps all of their speaking at once disturbed them.

Jesus' mission on earth, which had been put on hold for a few days, now continued in the power of the Holy Spirit. The same Spirit who had empowered Jesus now empowered His disciples. Simon Peter and the Eleven were no longer denying and running and hiding. In fact, in the power of God's Spirit, Simon, the reed, was becoming Peter, the rock. They stood up together before the crowd to explain what was happening and to proclaim Jesus Christ with new spiritual insight and power. Peter told the crowd they were witnessing the beginning of the fulfillment of the Joel 2:28, 29 prophecy. At this point, Peter did not quote Ezekiel or Jeremiah, who talked about the new heart and new spirit. Instead, Peter quoted Joel, who talked about the outpouring of the Spirit that would result in barriers being shattered in the realm of proclamation.

Peter interprets Joel's "It shall come to pass afterward" as "It shall come to pass in the last days" (Acts 2:17).

> The "last days" began with Christ's first advent and will end with His second advent; they are the days during which the age to come overlaps the present age. Hence the assurance with which Peter could quote the words of Joel and declare, "This is that."[4]

Peter quoted Joel 2:28-32. When this passage is studied in its original, historical context, it is an awesome reminder of God's consistency in dealing with His people. It is also an awesome reminder of the faithfulness of the all-wise God in giving promises and fulfilling them. The "afterward" in the original text marked an indefinite time, but what preceded the "afterward" shows the pattern of God's operation.

Because of the people's sins, God sent judgment (an army of locusts). The prophet urged the people to awaken and realize how desperate the situation was, and to turn fully to God, who perhaps would be gracious and forgive. After the lamenting and repenting, the people would be blessed with restoration—God would restore what had been destroyed. After spiritual restoration, a sure knowledge of the presence of God would be among them. After the knowledge of the presence of God, praises would replace lamentation and shame.

Then the "afterward" came, which Peter interpreted as "in the last days." The promise is that God would lavish His Spirit on His people. He would send a pouring out, a pouring forth, an abundance of His Spirit. The pouring out of God's Spirit would no longer be limited to leaders or a select few, but would be for *all* His people. The people of God would become a prophetic community. Barriers of gender, age, social status and ethnic background would be broken down by the operation of the Holy Spirit. All of these would experience "inspired utterance." Those on whom the Spirit was poured out would proclaim, and live in light of, the awesome Day of the Lord. In the pouring out of God's Spirit, these persons would be empowered to proclaim with clarity the good news of salvation through our Lord.

The rest of Peter's sermon presented basic truths about Jesus Christ. At the end of the message, the Holy Spirit brought conviction to the hearers, and they cried out, " 'Men and brethren, what shall we do?' Then Peter said to them, 'Repent, and let every one of you be baptized in the name of Jesus Christ for the remission of sins; and you shall receive the gift of the Holy Spirit'" (Acts 2:37, 38).

- First, was a call to repentance. Repentance is a change of mind, an abandoning of the old life and a turning fully in commitment to Jesus Christ. True repentance brings forgiveness of sins.

- Then the person is to demonstrate that commitment and forgiveness by being baptized according to the authority of Jesus Christ. Water baptism becomes a public declaration of allegiance to Jesus Christ. The forgiven, regenerated person will then receive the gift of the Holy Spirit.[5]

This message gave hope to the hearers, and about 3,000 were added to the church that day. The promise Peter gave about the Spirit is far-reaching: "For the promise is to you and to your children, and to all who are afar off, as many as the Lord our God will call" (v. 39). The promise of the Holy Spirit was not limited to the 120, but was offered to all those hearers. The promise did not stop with their generation, but reached to their descendants. The promise is to the Gentiles—those who are "afar off." The promise is available to all in every generation of every race—to everyone called by our Lord to salvation.

Acts 8

The impact of the outpouring of the Holy Spirit became evident in the believers' proclamation. They refused to be intimidated by persecution. Even when believers were driven out of Jerusalem, wherever they went they evangelized or proclaimed the good news about Jesus Christ. Philip, a man full of the Holy Spirit, went to Samaria and proclaimed Jesus Christ. The people heard Philip and saw the signs which accompanied his ministry. They believed in Jesus Christ and testified to their commitment through Christian baptism. The people experienced great joy. Simon, the sorcerer, also believed and was baptized.

When the apostles heard the news that Samaria had received the Word of God, they sent Peter and John, who went and prayed for them to receive the Holy Spirit. Although the people had received Christ as Lord, they had not received the baptism in the Holy Spirit: "For He had not yet fallen upon any of them" (Acts 8:16, *NASB*). Again, the metaphorical language communicates the power that comes from above suddenly and forcefully.[6]

Peter and John laid hands on the believers and they received the Holy Spirit. The accompanying evidence was so astonishing that Simon offered to buy the ability to lay hands on people for them to receive the Holy Spirit. Simon had been accustomed to having magical powers. He had witnessed signs, wonders and mighty works in Philip's ministry. After he believed and was baptized, he continued to be amazed at the mighty works of God. What he saw and/or heard when the Samaritans were baptized in the Holy Spirit was extraordinary. Scholars confidently conclude that "speaking in tongues" was the evidence observed.

F.F. Bruce said, "The context leaves us in no doubt that their reception of the Spirit was attended by external manifestations such as had marked His descent on the earliest disciples at Pentecost."[7]

Greek scholar A.T. Robertson said, "This participle (second aorist active of *horaô*) shows plainly that these who received the gift of the Holy Spirit spoke with tongues."[8]

Johannes Munck said, "Simon, who by virtue of his earlier life closely observed all wondrous faculties and powers, was struck by the apostles' ability to make the baptized prophesy and to speak in tongues by the laying on of hands."[9]

Acts 9

Saul of Tarsus, who had committed to Jesus Christ as Lord three days before, was communicating with the Lord and the Lord with him. The Lord was also communicating with Ananias about further ministry that Saul needed. Convinced that Saul was converted, Ananias went to him. Ananias laid his hands on Saul, and said, "Brother Saul, the Lord Jesus, who appeared to you on the road as you came, has sent me that you may receive your sight and be filled with the Holy Spirit" (Acts 9:17). Luke does not record Saul's speaking in tongues.

> In light of Paul's statement to the Corinthian church, "I thank God, I speak in tongues more than you all" (1 Corinthians 14:18, NASB), speaking in tongues must have been a part of his experience in Damascus. Luke's primary concern was with God's calling and empowering of Saul for his apostolic ministry. So Paul's experience was consistent with the

purpose of the outpouring of the Spirit on disciples at Pentecost and at Samaria. They, too, were equipped to bear the name of their Lord.[10]

Acts 10

The all-wise God was at work simultaneously in two men to prepare for a spiritual encounter. God was communicating with Peter so he would be prepared to receive Cornelius and his household as cleansed and accepted by God. God was also communicating with Cornelius to send for Peter and to be receptive to his message. The obedience of both men culminated in a great, spiritual outpouring. The atmosphere of receptivity was indicated by Cornelius' statement, "Now therefore, we are all present before God, to hear all the things commanded you by God" (Acts 10:33).

There were no supercritical attitudes. No prejudicial responses. No resistance to truth. Instead, there was a trust in God that He would supply the needs. There was an openness to God about how and through whom the answer would come. It is no wonder that while Peter was still preaching, "the Holy Spirit fell upon all those who heard the word. And those of the circumcision who believed were astonished, as many as came with Peter, because the gift of the Holy Spirit had been poured out on the Gentiles also. For they heard them speak with tongues and magnify God" (vv. 44-46).

Later, Peter and the six men of the circumcision who had witnessed the outpouring of the Holy Spirit at Cornelius' house went to Jerusalem to explain what happened. Peter rehearsed how God had confronted him and prepared him. Then Peter said,

> "And as I began to speak, the Holy Spirit fell upon them, as upon us at the beginning. Then I remembered the word of the Lord, how He said, 'John indeed baptized with water, but you shall be baptized with the Holy Spirit'" (11:15, 16).

"That tongues are the normative evidence of the baptism of the Spirit is unmistakably clear in this place. In fact, the Jewish believers who accompanied Peter knew that those Gentile converts had received the gift of the Holy Spirit, 'For they heard them speaking in tongues and magnifying God.'"[11]

Acts 19

Finding disciples at Ephesus, Paul asked them, "Did you receive the Holy Spirit [after] you believed?" (v. 2). He assumed they had believed. He knew that as believers they would have received the Spirit in regeneration. He did not assume that they had received the Spirit in the fullness of Charismatic power for witness. Paul assumed they would have a negative or an affirmative answer to the question—that they would know. He did not expect, "We hope so," "We think so," or "By faith we are assured." The point is that Paul expected them to have evidence, if they had been baptized in the Holy Spirit.

The Ephesians' answer indicated that they did not know that Holy Spirit power was being poured out on believers. Paul instructed them further, and they were baptized with Christian baptism. Paul then laid his hands on them and "the Holy Spirit came upon them, and they spoke with tongues and prophesied" (v. 6). A.T. Robertson said that "the speaking with tongues and prophesying was external and indubitable proof that the Holy Spirit had come on these twelve uninformed disciples now fully won to the service of Jesus as Messiah."[12]

ENDNOTES

[1] F.F. Bruce, *The Book of Acts* (Grand Rapids: Eerdmans, 1955) 54.

[2] Marvin Vincent, *Word Studies in the New Testament* (Wilmington, DE: Associated, 1972) 224.

[3] Bruce, 56.

[4] Bruce, 68.

[5] E.M. Blaiklock, *The Acts of the Apostles*, Tyndale New Testament Commentaries, ed. R.V.G. Tasker (Grand Rapids: Eerdmans, 1979) 60. "Repentance demands the witness of baptism: forgiveness is followed by the gift of the Holy Spirit."

Johannes Munck, *The Acts of the Apostles*, The Anchor Bible, eds. William Albright and David Freedman (Garden City, NY: Doubleday, 1967) 20. "Repent and let each of you be baptized, calling on the name of Jesus the Messiah, that your sins may be forgiven, and then you will receive the gift of the Holy Spirit."

[6] Rodman, 195.

[7] Bruce, 181.

[8] A.T. Robertson, *Word Pictures of the New Testament*, vol. 3 (New York: Harper and Brothers, 1932) 107.

[9] Johannes Munck, *The Acts of the Apostles*, The Anchor Bible, eds. William Albright and David Freedman (Garden City, NY: Doubleday, 1967) 75.

[10] Arrington, 100.

[11] Howard M. Ervin, *Spirit Baptism* (Peabody, MA: Hendrickson, 1987) 78, 79.

[12] Robertson, 313.

STUDY GUIDE
Lesson 5

Is speaking in tongues the pattern God set to indicate the entry into the Spirit-filled life? Was speaking in tongues the initial, or first, evidence of being baptized in the Holy Spirit in the accounts in the Book of Acts?

SCRIPTURES

"And they were all filled with the Holy Spirit and began to speak with other tongues, as the Spirit gave them utterance" (Acts 2:4).

"For the promise is to you and to your children, and to all who are afar off, as many as the Lord our God will call" (v. 39).

QUESTIONS AND READINGS

Read each of the following passages and complete the analysis of each.

Acts 2

1. Describe the characteristics of the disciples gathered in the Upper Room.

2. Contrast the Feast of Passover and the Feast of Pentecost.

3. What happened when the disciples were baptized in the Holy Spirit?

4. What was the response of the crowd?

5. What did Peter mean when he said, "This is that . . ." in reference to Joel 2:28-32?

6. What instructions and promise does Peter give in response to "What shall we do?"

Acts 8

7. What caused Philip to proclaim Jesus Christ in Samaria?

8. How did the people and Simon testify to their believing and accepting Jesus as Christ?

9. Describe the ministry of Peter and John in Samaria.

10. What happened when the disciples were baptized in the Holy Spirit?

Acts 9

11. Discuss the experience of Saul of Tarsus on the road to Damascus.

12. Discuss how God prepared Ananias for his ministry to Saul.

13. What happened in the encounter between Ananias and Saul?

Acts 10

14. Compare God's preparation of and directives to Cornelius with God's preparation of and directives to Peter.

15. Evaluate the atmosphere of receptivity in the gathering.

16. How did Peter and the other six Jewish men know that these had been baptized in the Holy Spirit?

Acts 19

17. What question did Paul ask the disciples at Ephesus?

18. What happened when these disciples were baptized in the Holy Spirit?

APPLICATION

In the Upper Room, the 120 were worshiping in faith, obedience and expectation when they were baptized in the Holy Spirit (Acts 2). At Samaria, Peter and John laid hands on the disciples and they were baptized in the Holy Spirit (ch. 8). Ananias laid hands on praying Saul and he was baptized in the Holy Spirit (ch. 9). Cornelius and his group were listening to the preaching of the Word when they were baptized in the Holy Spirit (ch. 10). Paul laid his hands on the disciples at Ephesus and they were baptized in the Holy Spirit (ch. 19). With these differences, the constant is that people were baptized in the Holy Spirit in an atmosphere of worship in obedience, faith and receptivity.

The overwhelming evidence is that speaking in tongues is the initial physical evidence of the baptism in the Holy Spirit.

Living in the Spirit

We have seen that Luke was intent on giving an accurate and orderly account of what God had done through Jesus Christ, and what God was continuing to do through Jesus' disciples. He emphasized that Jesus fulfilled His ministry in the power of the Holy Spirit. He also emphasized that the ministry of Jesus was being fulfilled in and through the disciples in the power of the Holy Spirit. He showed us that the hostile forces were greater than the disciples' abilities—except for the power of the Holy Spirit. Luke, the historian/theologian, gave us a story that shows the dynamic activity of the Holy Spirit in Jesus and in His disciples. The rapid spread of the gospel was directly attributable to the directing and empowering of the Holy Spirit. As the Holy Spirit directed and empowered Jesus, so He directs and empowers those who belong to Jesus.

In the accounts in Acts, the recurring phenomenon of speaking in other tongues as the Spirit gave the utterance accompanied the baptizing in the Holy Spirit. Speaking in tongues signaled the entrance into the Spirit-filled life. Speaking in tongues is shown to be the "initial evidence" of being baptized in the Holy Spirit.

Some have questioned the use of the word *evidence* because it gives "the impression of a modernistic (positivistic) preoccupation with empirical proof."[1] "Some are convinced that tongues as the initial 'sign' of Spirit baptism is a fruitful direction to follow."[2] The choice between "evidence" or "sign" would be a personal preference based on one's understanding of these terms.

God does not mislead us. Although the primary thrust of Acts is to emphasize the Spirit-filled, Spirit-led life, speaking in tongues is an integral part of the Spirit-filled life. There is no indication the pattern has changed.

Watson Mills suggested that tongues are an archaic symbolic expression, and that we should replace tongues with symbolic expressions that make more sense to the modern world. He suggested feeding the poor might be a useful symbolic expression.[3]

Some suggest love, but each of these expressions should result from regeneration. Speaking in tongues was not chosen nor sought by human beings; it was implemented by God. It was not a "faith tradition" that caused them to desire and expect tongues.

God has a way of choosing things that seem not to fit our human categories of thought very well. In Old Testament times "inspired utterance" indicated many times the coming of the Spirit on individuals. God's promise through Joel connected the outpouring of God's Spirit and "inspired utterance" or "inspired speech." Jesus had told the disciples to wait until they were clothed with power. Speaking in tongues marked their entry into a life of spiritual power, but their speaking in tongues was a source of witness as well.

Speaking in tongues at Cornelius' house was evidence to Peter and other Jewish witnesses that these Gentiles had entered fully into the Spirit-filled life. The speaking in tongues also broke down racial barriers. By the time Paul went to Ephesus and queried the 12 disciples with the question, "Did you receive the Holy Spirit after you believed?" he expected them to know.

After they spoke with tongues, no further questions were asked. It seems that one of the intentions in the details chosen for discussing this story in Acts is to show the pattern and norm for being baptized in the Holy Spirit.

Again, God does not mislead. Why do some not want to acknowledge speaking in tongues as the "initial evidence" of being baptized in the Holy Spirit?

- Is it because they are afraid of being accused of being "glosso-centric," or centered in tongues? The Spirit-filled life *is* the center.

- Is it because it is easier to be noncommittal in a pluralistic society?

- Is it because sometimes it is too controversial? To believe that Jesus Christ is the only way of salvation is controversial in a pluralistic society. One person challenged his pastor's sermon on John 14:6. He said he had a friend who was a good person, even though he did not accept Jesus; and he thought he would go to heaven.

- Is it because they, personally, have not spoken in tongues, so they assume it must not be the evidence?

- Is it because they assume their Christian friends who have not spoken in tongues are filled with the Spirit?

- Is it because they are afraid of being accused of spiritual arrogance? A truly Spirit-filled life is one of humility.

- Is it because they have never given a serious, open-hearted study to the Scriptural teaching and history?

- Is it because they have prayerfully, open-heartedly and thoroughly studied the Scriptures in their contexts, and are convinced that it is *not* the initial evidence?

If you have carefully read the previous pages in this book, you have found that speaking in tongues is dealt with in the context of the overall operations of the Holy Spirit. A particular blessing is singled out for discussion when neglect, ignorance, abuse, misinformation or resistance to it threatens to keep believers from experiencing the Holy Spirit-filled life.

We believe that when one pursues the baptizing in the Holy Spirit sincerely and receptively, speaking in tongues is the natural response to the overwhelming presence of God when one is baptized in the Holy Spirit.

Do not seek for tongues-speaking; rather, seek for Holy Spirit fullness with faith and receptivity. It seems that one reason this issue is not dealt with more in the Epistles is that it was generally accepted and practiced.

The directives given were correctives or further information. Notice two examples of general acceptance:

1. There was a general acceptance of which books of the Bible were sacred, but the Canon of Marcion and the Edict of Diocletian prompted an official fixing of the Canon, deciding officially which books were "Scriptures."

2. The deity of Christ was believed generally, but when Arius' sermons were confusing and drawing people into heresy, discussions and official statements at the Council of Nicea in A.D. 325 affirmed the deity of Christ.

In Scripture, when there is a problem with "inspired utterance," the issue is dealt with. For example, Paul said to the Thessalonians, "Do not quench the Spirit. Do not despise prophecies. Test all things; hold fast what is good" (1 Thessalonians 5:19-21). Further, Paul did not indicate surprise at believers' speaking in tongues at Corinth, but he addressed issues relating to it.

Speaking in tongues is not the whole of the Spirit-filled life, but the Sovereign Lord has chosen it to be an integral part. As the heaven of heavens cannot contain God, so we cannot contain the Holy Spirit. He contains us. He envelops us. He has us. We cannot describe an encounter with the Spirit; but when we try, we wind up with terms like *sudden, forceful, overwhelming, captivating, arresting, constraining, freeing, propelling, empowering, majestic, awe-inspiring,* and so forth. Yet, all of these terms pale into insignificance in our attempts to describe this divine-human encounter.

Perhaps one reason for speaking in tongues in this overwhelming encounter is that when human language fails, He gives us "inspired speech." The inspired speech does not transform us into great ones, because we do not originate the speech. Speaking His inspired speech reminds us of our frailty. In the presence of the transfigured Christ, Simon Peter did not know what to say . . . but he spoke anyway. God said, "This is My beloved Son, listen to Him!" (Mark 9:5-7, *NASB*).

Why struggle with limited human vocabulary when in that indescribable enveloping of the Holy Spirit's presence, He supplies the speech? To try to learn to speak in tongues is to cheapen the encounter. The Holy Spirit is free to speak or not to speak; we are free to be receptive and cooperate or to resist.

The Holy Spirit encounters us, as God encountered Moses on Mount Sinai. Moses had to be willing, obedient and receptive; and so must we. The Holy Spirit could "take over," but He does not. We speak as He directs. As we cannot control the wind, so we cannot control the Holy Spirit. When you are enveloped in the Holy Spirit, the experience is indescribable. The experience could be destructive, except that the Holy Spirit is the Spirit of Life. Rather than destroying, the Holy Spirit desires to infuse you with power, and govern that power for God's glory.

Speaking in tongues not only signals entrance into the Spirit-filled life, but it is a continuing ministry in and through the Spirit-filled person. The Scriptures reveal truths concerning this.

- A person speaking in tongues is speaking mysteries to God (1 Corinthians 14:2). No one understands what is spoken. He who speaks in tongues is built up spiritually (v. 4).

- Speaking in tongues surpasses our limited language to articulate praises acceptably to God (see v. 17).

- Speaking in tongues is available to every believer. Otherwise, why would Paul say, "I wish you all spoke with tongues, but even more that you prophesied" (v. 5). Paul expressed his wish that all would speak in tongues. He then amplified his wish by saying that in addition, he wished all would prophesy so that the church could be built up.

- Speaking in tongues is a reminder that these are the "last days" (Acts 2:17). This reminder should prompt us to live in Holy Spirit fullness so that we, with a sense of urgency and spiritual power, proclaim the gospel of Jesus Christ. Being baptized in the Holy Spirit and speaking in tongues break down racial, social and cultural barriers (Acts 10; 11).

Note another ministry of the Holy Spirit: "Likewise the Spirit helps us in our weakness; for we do not know how to pray as we ought, but that very Spirit intercedes with sighs too deep for words. And God, who searches the heart, knows what is the mind of the Spirit, because the Spirit intercedes for the saints according to the will of God" (Romans 8:26, 27, NRSV).

We identify with the brokenness of our world. We lament. In awe before the mystery of divine operations and in agony before the human dilemma, we attempt to articulate the impossible. The Holy Spirit, knowing the perfect will of God and the needs we face, takes hold with us and through inarticulate sounds, He articulates our concerns.[4]

We give voice to the cry of the Holy Spirit on behalf of the broken and oppressed. This is not empty grieving, but grieving that is healing. It is a cry that is answered. The Holy Spirit supersedes our inabilities to understand and put into words the prayers needed. That which is humanly inexpressible is inexplicably expressed through us by the Holy Spirit.

KEEP ON BEING FILLED

Paul said, "And be not drunk with wine, in which is debauchery, but keep on being filled in the Spirit, speaking to yourselves in psalms and hymns and spiritual songs, singing and psalming with your heart to the Lord, giving thanks always for all things in the name of our Lord Jesus Christ, even to God, our Father. Being subject to one another in the fear of Christ" (Ephesians 5:18-21, author's translation).

It is the will of God for each believer to be baptized in the Holy Spirit and to keep on being filled with the Holy Spirit. Rather than allowing your life to be controlled or governed by an intoxicant, keep on allowing your life to be controlled or governed by the Holy Spirit. The Holy Spirit will lead you to experience God's provisions.

One example of this on-going filling is found in Acts 4. Because of the miracle of healing recorded in Acts 3, and the subsequent preaching, teaching, and salvations, the religious hierarchy were stirred to action. Peter and John were arrested and imprisoned. The next day, Peter and John were arraigned for questioning. They were asked, "By what power or by what name did you do this?" (Acts 4:7). Luke then indicates the source of Peter's boldness of response, "Then Peter, filled with the Holy Spirit, said to them ... " (Acts 4:8). Peter proclaimed Jesus.

The religious leaders were greatly impressed by the boldness of Peter and John because they knew they were not formally educated and that they were considered laymen or common men with no officially authorized titles. The evidence that they were connected to Jesus and that Divine power operated in their lives was irrefutable.

The religious leaders threatened, commanded, and charged Peter and John not to speak or teach at all in the name of Jesus. These Spirit-filled disciples recognized their continuing need of Divine power so they would not be intimidated by the enemy. When they were released, they went to their own spiritual companions and shared the new challenges. They prayed together, asking God for boldness to continue to proclaim His Word in the face of threatening. "And they were all filled with the Holy Spirit, and spoke the Word of God with boldness" (Acts 4:31).

The Acts 4 example illuminates the need of the command "keep on being filled with the Holy Spirit." The disciples did not wait for a spiritual lapse or a spiritual low. They had been proclaiming God's Word with boldness, and they wanted to continue proclaiming God's Word with boldness.

The Holy Spirit-baptized person can continue to be filled with the Spirit so that each new challenge is faced not merely with human strength but in the power of the Holy Spirit.

Many ongoing benefits result from the Spirit-filled, Spirit-empowered life. The Holy Spirit-filled life is characterized by a fullness of inner joy. You will sing and make melody in your heart. An attitude of thankfulness will pervade your life. Mutual building up and mutual encouragement flow from Spirit-led lives. Worship of the Lord is enhanced in the Spirit-filled life. Barriers in the body of Christ are broken down and trust prevails, so that mutual submission is practiced among Spirit-filled brothers and sisters.

In the Spirit-filled life, our character and conduct are governed by the Holy Spirit. He is the Spirit of Holiness, and He empowers us to live the holy life. Christlikeness is continually produced in us by the Spirit.

According to the accounts in Acts, the baptism in the Holy Spirit was not received by those who were complacent and closed, but by the spiritually desirous and open believers. Spirit baptism was not received by the arrogant nor the argumentative, but by persons acknowledging their need, and praying and seeking God.

May we pursue Spirit-fullness. In the Spirit-filled life, we will emphasize the centrality of Jesus Christ, prayer, the Word of God, sensitivity to the Spirit, and evangelistic outreach.

Some seem fearful that to have a theology of the Spirit is to diminish the role of Jesus. There is no competition in the Trinity, however. The Son reveals the Father. The Son testifies to the coming of the Holy Spirit. The Father and the Son send the Holy Spirit. The Holy Spirit testifies of Jesus Christ and administers the provisions of the incarnate, cruci-fied, risen and ascended Lord.

To seek Spirit baptism does not diminish regener-ation nor the lordship of Jesus Christ. To seek Spirit baptism actually submits to the lordship of Jesus because He shows us the importance of living in Holy Spirit fullness. May we experience continually the fullness of the Holy Spirit, so that the ministry of Jesus continues through us, directed and empow-ered by the Spirit's presence.

ENDNOTES

[1] Frank D. Macchia, "Groans Too Deep for Words: Towards the Theology of Tongues as Initial Evidence," online, <http://www.apts.edu/ajps/98-2/98-2-macchia.htm> cited 03 May 1999.

[2] Macchia, "Groans Too Deep For Words" online.

[3] Watson Mills, "A Theological Interpretation of Tongues in Acts and 1 Corinthians," diss., Southern Baptist Theological Seminary, 1968, 224, 225.

[4] Macchia, "Sighs Too Deep for Words," *Journal of Pentecostal Theology* 1 (1992): 59. Macchia has some helpful comments concerning Romans 8:26, 27: "Most Pentecostals have rightly understood glosso-lalia as the 'sighs (groanings) too deep for words' in Romans 8:26. They have not been alone in this inter-pretation. Origen and Chrysostom are the earliest commentators found tying tongues to Romans 8:26. Modern scholars such as Hermann Gunkel, Julius Schniewind, Ernst Käsemann, Krister Stendahl, and John A.T. Robinson have also interpreted Romans 8:26 as a reference to glossolalia."

STUDY GUIDE
Lesson 6

Since speaking in tongues is the first evidence of the baptism in the Holy Spirit, what are other evidences or results of the Spirit-filled life? What does it mean to "keep on being filled with the Holy Spirit"?

SCRIPTURES

"And be not drunk with wine, in which is debauchery, but keep on being filled in the Holy Spirit, speaking to yourselves in psalms and hymns and spiritual songs, singing and psalming with your heart to the Lord, giving thanks always for all things in the name of the Lord Jesus Christ even to God, our Father. Being subject to one another in the fear of Christ" (see Ephesians 5:18-21).

QUESTIONS AND READINGS

1. Is speaking in tongues the initial evidence of being baptized in the Holy Spirit just for certain "faith traditions," or is it the normative Biblical sign provided by God for every Christian?

2. In addition to speaking in tongues as the initial evidence of being baptized in the Holy Spirit, what are other blessings and meanings indicated in Scripture of speaking in tongues?

3. Discuss the difference in seeking tongues-speaking or seeking Holy Spirit fullness.

4. Explain the unique and powerful way the Holy Spirit helps us in prayer according to Romans 8:26, 27.

5. What is the meaning of "Keep on being filled with the Holy Spirit"?

APPLICATION

Living in Holy Spirit fullness is the God-intended life. Jesus Christ made complete provisions for us so that we might live godly lives, pray effectively, and witness in the power of the Holy Spirit. As believers, we desire all God has for us so we can become all He wants us to be and do all He wants us to do. After we have been baptized in His Holy Spirit, we want to obey the command to keep on being filled with the Spirit.

Part III
Historical Evidence

Montanist to the Shakers

Eighteen hundred years of church history separate the end of the first-century church and the dramatic outpouring of the Holy Spirit in what we know as the Azusa Street Revival (Los Angeles, 1906-1909). What happened during this massive expanse of time? Did Spirit baptism and the demonstration of tongues cease to exist? Absolutely not!

Did the spiritual gifts, as well as Spirit baptism, lie dormant until a "spiritual springtime" caused them to blossom in the lives of believers and congregations? Again we respond with a resounding "No way!" Various forces did invade the church, however, diminishing the light of the gospel and inhibiting the moving of the Holy Spirit.

The desire to organize fosters a dependency on

human actions rather than relying on the spontaneous guidance of the Spirit. Too frequently shepherds of the flock are enticed and become entrapped with greed for possessions and power. They become self-servers rather than Christ's servants. As a result, the spirituality of the church suffers. Just as devastating is the general complacency that creeps in, causing individuals to assume their goodness and slide along in a form of godliness based on words and outward ceremony.

But God isn't limited by one or a combination of these circumstances! When individuals and/or groups desire spiritual fullness, the Holy Spirit bursts into their lives with dimensions far beyond the "status quo" of the church and religious life that surrounds them. Not only are they thrust into new experiences of life in the Spirit, but they suddenly are alienated from their contemporaries who at best assume them to be misled, and at worst to be crazed or demonized.

A review of the centuries that followed the founding of the church indicates periods of spiritual darkness so thick and oppressive that one wonders how any light could exist, much less pierce through it. It seemed that surely the church was in its death throes. Then we read of beams of spiritual light poking holes in the clouds of darkness. The Holy Spirit baptized believers, empowered them to speak in tongues and prophesy, provided miraculous healings, and enabled them to illuminate their communities.

Interestingly, these people were neither perfect in their practices nor always within the borders of orthodox theology and Biblical interpretation. First Timothy 4:16 admonishes us, "Watch your life and doctrine closely. Persevere in them, because if you do, you will save both yourself and your hearers" (*NIV*). If God were to use perfection and normalcy as the criteria for spiritual blessing, however, none of us would ever experience the fullness of His Spirit. If God were to use the standard of spiritual maturity for His continued blessings, few individuals and organizations would ever grow out of infancy.

These concepts are not excuses for false doctrine and aberrant actions, but they do indicate why we find some unusual ideas and activities among individuals who are experiencing the fullness of the Holy Spirit. We need to consider briefly some of the factors that frequently push individuals and groups beyond the borders of Biblical theology and lifestyle.

First is the well-known "pendulum effect." Seeking to rectify wrongs in a body causes many to swing past the center position and move too far in the other direction. For example, a group concerned over the acceptance of sinful actions may swing to forms of legalism in their attempt to bring wholeness to the church.

Second in our list of causes is the lack of accountability. This is seen when one or several individuals press for spiritual renewal, but in the process there is no one to say "wait a minute" when excesses occur. The sounder of the alert must have both the responsibility and authority within the setting.

Thirdly, a frequent contributor is the concept of valuing experience above Scripture. This will be discussed in a later chapter, but a brief statement seems appropriate here. When experiences are not examined in the lens of Scripture, any number of interpretations become possible. Also, the enthusiasm of the moment seems to color one's thinking rather than allowing an unbiased perspective.

Closely tied to the previous cause is the fourth one—claims of receiving a divine message or messenger. Too frequently other believers feel obligated to simply accept what someone says has come from God by the Holy Spirit. In doing so, they bind their ability to ask analyzing questions within the realm of faith. Truth will always stand the test of honest searching questions. When leaders refuse to be questioned and followers choose not to question, the stage is set for spiritual bondage that may result in heresy, immoral actions and, on occasion, spiritual or even physical death.

This chapter provides some brief glimpses of Spirit baptism and tongues from the second century to the beginning of the 20th century. The aim is not to be comprehensive. Other authors and volumes will supply the "rest of the story." Our purpose is to reflect the continuity of the experience even when not endorsed by the established churches of those centuries and when lacking a distinctly Pentecostal theology. The examples given will emphasize groups rather than isolated incidents or individuals. Although there are many of those, it seems important to understand the breadth of those experiencing the work of the Holy Spirit and, specifically, tongues.

THE MONTANISTS

As the first-century church expanded, it faced problems of disunity and heresy. These problems never seem to be eradicated from God's people. When our Enemy cannot stop the progress of the church from the outside through persecution, he resorts to disruption from within. In attempting to combat these problems, two bishops offered solutions that would later be seen by some as placing too much emphasis on human leadership rather than Spirit guidance. Writing to the Corinthian church about A.D. 95, Clement, bishop of Rome, advocated obedience to the local bishop as a guarantee to unity. Fifteen years later, Ignatius, bishop of Antioch in Syria, wrote to various churches and advocated subjection to their bishops as a means for unity and for avoiding heresy.

In the middle of the second century (after A.D. 155), under the leadership of Montanus, a concern arose that the church was becoming too formal in its worship and was too man-oriented rather than Spirit-led. He and others of like mind wanted the spontaneous moving of the Holy Spirit in worship and more divine leadership. Dominant in the Montanist Movement was the gift of prophecy. They claimed to be the "latter rain," in contrast to first-century Pentecost. A strong emphasis on the gift of prophecy caused them to see their prophecies as infallible truth, even when they were not in agreement with the whole truth of the Bible.[1]

The existence of tongues within the Montanist Movement cannot be overlooked. While not specifically naming them, it is generally believed that both Irenaeus and Tertullian referred to the Montanists and the practice of tongues. In the latter half of the second century, Irenaeus, bishop of Lyons, in *Against Heresies*, included a valuable detail in this work against the Gnostics:

> In like manner we do also hear many brethren in the church, who possess prophetic gifts, and

who through the Spirit speak all kinds of languages, and bring to light for the general benefit the hidden things of men, and declare the mysteries of God.[2]

Tertullian, an African theologian, spoke with an insider's view, since he became a Montanist for a number of years. While not naming the Montanists, his words offer insight about the existence of tongues in his work, *Against Marcion*. The following is a brief excerpt:

Let Marcion then exhibit, as gifts of his god, some prophets, such as have not spoken by human senses, but with the Spirit of God, such as have both predicted things to come, and have made manifest the secrets of the heart; let him produce a psalm, a vision, a prayer—only let it be by the Spirit, in our ecstasy; that is, in rapture, whenever an interpretation of tongues has occurred to him.[3]

In the event neither Irenaeus nor Tertullian are referring to the Montanists, their historical writings emphasize the continuance of tongues after the era of the apostolic church. Besides, they aren't the only historical sources of the second and third centuries. Origen, an Alexandrian theologian, records the complaint of the pagan philosopher, Celsus. Speaking of the Palestinian Christians he stated,

"To these promises are added strange, fanatical and quite unintelligible words."[4] How often have we heard such statements by those who do not understand or believe in the operation of tongues through the Holy Spirit?

THE CAMISARDS—PROPHETS OF THE CÉVENNES

When Martin Luther issued his *Ninety-five Theses*, little did he realize the forces that would eventually be unleashed. Part of the story is the persecution as well as the battles that were fought by and against the Protestants. Between 1559 and 1598, the French Protestants, known as the Huguenots, were involved in eight wars and the infamous St. Bartholomew Massacre. Finally, in 1598 the Edict of Nantes provided a toleration and freedom for their theology and practice. Less than a century later, however, the tables were reversed as Louis XIV revoked the edict as part of his plan for absolute uniformity in the kingdom.

The Huguenots faced a decision on how to respond. "In those valleys of southern France which had enjoyed liberty of worship for a full human lifetime, resentment was hot against the representatives of the government.[5] They chose to endorse resistance against King Louis and wage bloody warfare (1702-1705) in an effort to restore the church. They became known as the Prophets of the Cévennes (region) or the Camisards. The former reflects their prophetic emphasis and the geographic location, while the latter refers to "the jacket which they wore over their clothes during the night raids."[6]

Apparently this group never numbers more than 5,000, but the intensity for their beliefs becomes very evident in battle. It is described as "fighting" with brutal fury, even when they marched into battle with psalms on their lips, while the royal troops punished them with torture and imprisonment.[7]

The Camisards believed a greater fulfillment of Joel's prophecy than seen in the Book of Acts could be expected.[8] Speaking in tongues was one of the prominent manifestations. Some spoke in tongues for as long as two hours. Being greeted by a holy kiss became one method of receiving the baptism of the Spirit.[9]

Speaking in tongues continued in England among the direct descendants of the Camisards.

Small English children were heard to speak in fluent French, some carried on two- and three-way conversations in an unknown tongue. Some were heard to speak intelligently in Latin, Hebrew and Greek when they knew, at the most, a few isolated phrases.[10]

The accounts of other extreme phenomena are interesting and informational. People would fall from heights of up to 12 feet with no physical

injury. Sharp knives driven into their bodies produced no pain, injury or after-effect. Fire would
not burn them during these special manifestations
of the Holy Spirit.

THE JANSENISTS

France provided the geographic environment for
another group in which a dynamic manifestation of
spiritual gifts occurred. The Jansenist Movement
takes its name from Dutch theologian Cornelius
Jansen, who later became the bishop of Ypres. It can
be described as an Evangelical Movement within
the Roman Catholic Church of the 1600s and early
1700s. It originated in a controversy over the doctrine of grace, reducing the significance of the
Roman Catholic Church as earthly mediator
between God and man. The Society of Jesus
(Jesuits) persecuted the Jansenists "for speaking in
tongues, prophesying, discerning spirits, and praying for the sick."[11]

Though the Jansenists attempted to separate
themselves from the temptations and distractions
of the world, they did not refuse all contact with
the world. Their spirituality included performing
good works and acts of charity toward the poor
and unfortunate.[12]

Many substantial miracles occurred within the
movement. This became a powerful apologetic,

and helped deflect some of the suspicions that arose. One miracle of special importance was the cure of Marguerita Perrier, the niece of the well-known philosopher and mathematician, Blaise Pascal.

On March 24, 1656, a consecrated thorn was touched to her disfiguring eye sore, and the eye was suddenly healed. This is just one of many dramatic healings that are documented.

It appears that glossolalia (speaking in tongues) was quite common in the latter portion of the movement's history. Many of the Jansenists, known as "convulsionaries," due to the unusual motor phenomena, had a "feeling that the Holy Spirit was present within them and a sense of direct communication with God," as a result of this Scriptural manifestation.[13]

THE SHAKERS

Roots of the Shakers are found within the traditions of the English Quakers and English Camisards. Having already considered the Camisards, a brief note concerning the Quakers is added here. The practice of tongues was seen in the early years of Quakerism. One of them records:

> We received after the pouring down of the
> Spirit upon us, and our hearts were made
> glad and our tongues loosed and our

mouths opened, and we spake with new
tongues as the Lord gave utterance.[14]

George Fox, their founder, discouraged these
more spectacular gifts, however, and eventually
they were no longer evident.

Controversial Ann Lee Stanley, later referred to
as Mother Ann Lee, was the initiator and leader of
the Shakers. She claimed to be the daughter of God
in the Spirit, and the female counterpart to Jesus.
During an imprisonment, she further claimed to
have received a revelation of the "mystery of iniq-
uity," being sexual intercourse. Stressing complete
chastity, the imminent return of Christ, a pure form
of communal living and the allegorical interpretation of Scripture resulted in her followers being
separated from English church circles. On the basis
of a revelation directing them to go to America,
Ann Lee, eight other adults and three small children migrated to the American colonies, landing in
New York City on August 6, 1774.[15]

Of special emphasis is their interest in the resti-
tution of the gifts of the Spirit within the church.[16]
Speaking in tongues along with prophesying,
singing, dancing, shaking and shouting became a
regular part of their worship.[17]

Apparently the gift of tongues was not a gift of
an exclusive few. "Although converts initially
encountered it as a sign of the operation of the

Holy Spirit, it soon became a part of their normal experience."[18]

The extent of the Shaker community with its practices and beliefs needs to be noted. At its height there were 24 separate communities, spanning from the New England states to as far west as Kentucky and Indiana and as far south as Florida. The peak was prior to the Civil War when there were about 6,000 adherents.

ENDNOTES

[1] Bernard L. Bresson, *Studies in Ecstasy* (New York: Vantage, 1966) 28.

[2] Donald Lee Barnett and Jeffrey P. McGregor, *Speaking in Other Tongues: A Scholarly Defense* (Seattle: Community Chapel, 1986) 231.

[3] Barnett and McGregor, 231.

[4] Barnett and McGregor, 236.

[5] R.A. Knox, *Enthusiasm: A Chapter in the History of Religion* (New York: Oxford, 1950) 357.

[6] *The New Schaff-Herzog Encyclopedia of Religious Knowledge* (Grand Rapids: Baker) 368.

[7] Ibid, 369.

[8] Michael P. Hamilton, ed., *The Charismatic Movement* (Grand Rapids: Eerdmans, 1975) 75.

[9] Bresson, 42.

[10] Bresson, 56.

[11] Bresson, 239.

[12] B. Robert Kreiser, *Miracles, Convulsions, and Ecclesiastical Politics in Early Eighteenth-Century Paris* (Princeton: Princeton UP, 1978) 86.

[13] Kreiser, 268.

[14] Bresson, 68.

[15] Bresson, 72.

[16] Hamilton, 82.

[17] Bresson, 76.

[18] Hamilton, 83.

STUDY GUIDE
Study Lesson 7

Why should we be aware of the continuance of Spirit baptism and the demonstration of tongues after the New Testament era? There are numerous examples of individuals and groups who experienced Spirit baptism and tongues from the second century until the marvelous Azusa Street Revival beginning in 1906. They continue to validate the prophecies of the past, promising this experience for all. These examples also demonstrate there is no truth to the concept of tongues ceasing to exist after the first century.

SCRIPTURES

First Timothy 4:16 is quoted in your text using the *New International Version*. Look up the verse in a different translation to further grasp its meaning and significance. Then answer the following:

1. How much importance have I given to knowing and living out the basic doctrines of the Bible?

2. What possible differences may be evident in my life by giving greater emphasis specifically to the doctrine of the Holy Spirit and speaking in tongues as the initial evidence?

Look up 1 Corinthians 14:40 and write it in your study guide.

How might you apply this verse to the worship of your local congregations as well as your personal actions of life in the Spirit?

To fully understand its impact, remember the context of this verse is one of spiritual gifts operating in a worship service. It reminds us that even what may appear unusual will be orderly, if operated according to God's design.

Historically, and even currently, we see some individuals who, due to their lack of doctrinal/Biblical information and complacency, may be caught up in actions or activities that are not Spirit-led. They may be sincere and mean well, but it still demonstrates a pattern that isn't acceptable.

QUESTIONS AND READINGS

Read the pages that are assigned for this lesson and answer the following questions.

1. What are three forces that invade the church and diminish the light of the gospel?

2. List four factors that may cause individuals, as well as groups, to go beyond the borders of Biblical theology and lifestyle.

3. What was Montanus' desire for the church?

4. How do the Camisards perceive speaking in tongues?

5. What are some of the claims and beliefs of Ann Lee Stanley, founder of the Shakers?

6. Which two groups covered in this section originated in France?

PERSONAL PERSPECTIVE

Up to this point of the historical review, what person or event stands out to you? Why?

Irvingites to the Parhamites

The Irvingites differ greatly from any of the other groups considered up to this point. First, the preaching of their pastor, Edward Irving, drew large numbers of influential leaders to his church. George Channing, who later became the prime minister, promoted this man's preaching. Frequently, 1,000 to 1,500 people attempted to squeeze into the 500-seat Caledonian Chapel.[1]

Second, they had a distinct Pentecostal theology which stated that speaking in tongues is the initial evidence of the Holy Spirit baptism.

Central to all this is the person of Edward Irving, a Church of Scotland minister, whose ministry blossomed in London, England. Irving's desire for true spirituality could be seen early in his life. When he was 12 years old, rather than attend the national church in his hometown of Annan,

Scotland, he would walk six miles on Sunday to attend a Seceder church in a nearby village.[2]

After graduating from the University of Edinburgh at age 17 with a master of arts, it was 14 years before he became a senior pastor. The reason for this, it is said, was because he was unwilling to "brownnose" the elders of various congregations who were responsible for calling ministers when a vacancy occurred.

At a ministerial conference in 1825, Irving heard an Anglican pastor testify of "seeking for the out-pouring of the promised latter rain spoken of by Joel."[3] He was deeply challenged. Three years later, he met A.J. Scott. Scott believed that the *charismata* of the apostles "had been lost to the church only because of coldness of heart and lack of faith . . . they had never been withdrawn and were still available as in the days of Peter and Paul."[4]

Edward Irving was the first person to project speaking in tongues to be the initial evidence of Spirit baptism. This is a step beyond the centuries of thought that viewed tongues only as one of the gifts of the Spirit. Irving left no doubt when he was quoted in *Pentecost* magazine as believing a person does not have the Holy Ghost at all unless he speaks with tongues.[5] His first mention of a special outpouring of the Spirit in the near future as prophesied in the Scriptures (the latter rain) was in the preface to *The Coming of Christ in Glory*, a book which he translated.[6]

As more and more of his congregation received the Spirit baptism with the evidence of tongues, Irving faced the issue of whether to allow it in church services. Initially, he forbade tongues in the regular service, but allowed it in the early morning prayer services.

Eventually, he opened two segments in the regular service where tongues could be exercised. Tongues were first heard on Sunday, October 16, 1831. Over 1,500 were in attendance in the new worship sanctuary. On the next Sunday, 4,000 squeezed into the sanctuary, but no tongues were heard.[7]

On Sunday, October 30, 1831, Irving preached a sermon titled "The Gift of Tongues Enjoyed in the Church." He emphasized the continuance of the ministry of the Spirit in the church.

> Many have seen that these gifts ought to be
> in the church always, were intended to be in
> the church always. Was not the Holy Ghost
> promised to everyone that believeth? Was
> he not promised as the Comforter, that was
> to abide forever?[8]

Besides believing in tongues as the standing sign or initial evidence of Spirit baptism, Irving also perceived those who spoke in tongues as being on a higher spiritual level. Probably because he had not spoken in tongues, he placed himself in submission to those leaders in his church who had.

Irving was removed from being the pastor of Caledonian Chapel on May 2, 1832, because he allowed tongues in the church to be spoken by women and those who had not been ordained. A statement he made nearly 70 years before Charles Fox Parham, became a tenet of belief in the 20th-century Pentecostal Movement in the United States. In his volume titled *Day of Pentecost: On the Baptism of the Holy Ghost*, Irving wrote, "The baptism of the Holy Ghost, whose standing sign, if we err not, is speaking with tongues."[9]

GROUPS PRIOR TO AZUSA STREET

We now come to a junction where it becomes necessary to cast a broad view. In the 1890s a number of groups across the United States experienced speaking in tongues and came to the conclusion that it was the same experience recorded in the Book of Acts.

In the Church of God, the Shearer Schoolhouse Revival of 1896 became a special focal point. It began with families gathering for prayer in Cherokee County, North Carolina. Into this isolated geographic area with its fertile spiritual environment came three men sharing the distinctives of a sanctification experience. The presentation of the doctrine of holiness, coupled with the condition of spiritual starvation, produced a marvelous spiritual renewal. People heard of it and began traveling 20 and 30 miles in difficult mountainous terrain to be a part of this renewal in Cherokee County, North Carolina. The specific location was Camp Creek.

While engaging in fervent prayer, individuals of both genders and various ages began to speak in languages unknown to them. Not having any previous knowledge of such occurrences, it wasn't until searching the Scriptures that they came to the conclusion that this was like the Day of Pentecost (Acts 2). At this point there was no clearly defined doctrine of the Spirit and a distinct concept of initial evidence. Of special importance was their seeing tongues as a sign of Spirit baptism and not just one of the possible signs of sanctification.[10]

Pentecostal experiences in the 1890s were also occurring among non-English speaking immigrants in the United States. In his book, *Northern Harvest: Pentecostalism in North Dakota*, Darrin Rodgers shares extensive reports of speaking in tongues among Swedish and Norwegian settlers in the Dakotas, Minnesota and Canada.

Evangelist Carl M. "Daddy" Hanson was one of the spiritual fathers of Pentecostals in the northern Great Plains. Although he did not receive Spirit baptism with the evidence of speaking in tongues until 1899, he became familiar with individuals who had experienced this phenomena in his meetings. The first occasion occurred in 1895. When a small girl began speaking in tongues, he declared it to be what had been spoken of by the prophet Joel. This Norwegian minister was both a pre-Azusa and post-Azusa Pentecostal.[11]

Under the pastoral ministry of John Thompson, a Swedish Free Mission pastor, there were Pentecostal manifestations in the years prior to Azusa Street. Since there was a protracted revival prior to the manifestation of tongues and other spiritual gifts, conflicting reports make it difficult to place an exact date. It is safe to say, however, that this outpouring occurred during the period of 1899 to 1903. Darrin Rodgers includes an excerpt written by Thompson's son describing the revival:

> God graciously poured out His Spirit with signs following. Many received the glorious Baptism in the Holy Ghost speaking in other tongues as the Spirit of God gave utterance. At that time we had not heard of any other places having received a like experience, but later we heard of people in California and Winnipeg, Canada, having received a like precious outpouring of the Holy Spirit.[12]

A single sentence from Rodger's book provides the perspective for what took place in the Great

Plains region in the pre-Azusa years: "In Minnesota and the Dakotas, scattered reports of tongues-speech exist from 1885 to 1899, followed by documentation of more that a dozen tongues-speaking congregations from 1899 to 1906."[13]

THE PARHAMITES

Charles Fox Parham stands as a pivotal figure in the Pentecostal Movement. Often referred to as the "Father of the Formally Stated Pentecostal Doctrine," he provides the foundation of belief which eventually breaks out in the Azusa Street Revival and spreads to the far reaches of the world. This man "was one of those who believed that if the complacent, prosperity-ridden, coldly formalistic church and its members were to be reached, an enduement of the Spirit would be necessary."[14]

Parham's personal life provides an interesting foundation for the ministry that developed. In college he became a backslider, and decided to become a physician. During a severe illness that took him near death, Parham responded positively to God's question, "Will you preach?" He experienced healing except for his ankles, and this required his learning to walk on the sides of his feet. Later, God healed his ankles. He renewed his vow to God to preach, even offering to quit college and go into the ministry.[15]

Initially, Parham served as a Congregational lay preacher. Later, he associated with the Methodists. His view of the destruction of the wicked and especially his not insisting on converts joining the church resulted in his leaving the Methodists and joining the growing Holiness Movement.

When God healed Parham from severe heart disease, this prompted the Parham family to give up medicines, doctors and life insurance. They established Bethel Healing Home, a divine healing home, in Topeka, Kansas, in 1898. Here, individuals seeking healing were provided home-like comforts while surrounded by others of like faith and prayer.

Parham's opening of Bethel Bible College in October 1900 set the stage for the doctrine and practice of tongues as the initial evidence of the baptism of the Holy Spirit. He held two distinct beliefs about tongues. First, Parham believed that the Acts 2 account is a gift of languages that would enable individuals to push back language barriers in missionary outreach and preach. Second, he was convinced of an experience after sanctification that is evidenced by speaking in tongues.

Before leaving for Kansas City in late December 1900, Parham left his students an assignment. They were to individually study the Scriptures and conclude whether or not there is a special witness or evidence of a person's having received

Spirit baptism. On his return they all concluded that speaking in tongues is the outward sign. The confirmation of this conclusion came when 70 outsiders and 40 students gathered for a "watch-night" service.[16] In the early hours of January 1, 1901—the first day of the 20th century—one of the students, Agnes N. Ozman, received the baptism in the Holy Spirit.

It was after midnight . . . when Miss Ozman began "speaking in the Chinese language" while a "halo seemed to surround her head and face." Following the experience, Ozman was unable to speak in English for three days, and when she tried to communicate by writing she invariably wrote in Chinese character.[17]

During the month of January, classes were suspended as the entire student body and faculty sought for Spirit baptism. Parham received the baptism on the night of January 3, 1901, after many students had experienced the same Spirit baptism.

The tremendous significance of this outpouring of the Holy Spirit in Topeka is the projection of speaking in tongues being the outward sign, or evidence, of Spirit baptism. Tongues were seen as separate from one of the possible signs of sanctification or as a spiritual gift. Now tongues stood as proof of the baptism in the Holy Spirit.

Despite what took place, Parham and his fellow believers faced difficult times in the first several years. People, generally, did not accept this new doctrine and experience. No breakthrough occurred until the fall of 1903, when a three-month revival took place in Galena, Kansas. The *Cincinnati Inquirer* reported over 1,000 people healed and 800 converted. From this point, small groups of Pentecostals spread out into other states—Missouri, Texas and Florida. "It is estimated that by the winter of 1905, Texas alone had 25,000 Pentecostal believers and about 60 preachers—all the direct result of Parham's consecrated efforts."[18]

Although the Pentecostal doctrine and experience received a foundation and some initial building steps through Parham's ministry, the spiritual explosion came when a student, W.J. Seymour, took the message to Los Angeles in 1906. This will be discussed in the next chapter.

Before leaving the Parhamites, it must be noted that Charles F. Parham's view of tongues as the initial evidence of the baptism in the Holy Spirit had no connection to Edward Irving's view. It developed independently, separated by the Atlantic Ocean and 70 years of historical time.

ENDNOTES

[1] Arnold Dallimore, *The Life of Edward Irving: Forerunner of the Charismatic Movement* (Carlisle, PA: The Banner of Truth Trust, 1983) 40.

[2] Dallimore, 11.

[3] Barnett and McGregor, 244.

[4] Dallimore, 87.

[5] Bresson, 96.

[6] Dallimore, 88.

[7] William S. Merricks, *Edward Irving: The Forgotten Giant* (East Peoria, IL: Scribe's Chamber Publications, 1983) 187.

[8] Merricks, 194.

[9] Merricks, 223.

[10] Charles W. Conn, *Like a Mighty Army* (Cleveland: Pathway, 1996) 29.

[11] Darrin Rodgers, *Northern Harvest: Pentecostalism in North Dakota* (Bismarck: North Dakota District Council of the Assemblies of God, 2003) 6-12.

[12] Rodgers, 12.

[13] Rodgers, 13.

[14] John Thomas Nichol, *Pentecostalism* (New York: Harper and Row, 1966) 26.

[15] Sarah E. Parham, *The Life of Charles F. Parham: Founder of the Apostolic Movement* (New York: Garland, 1985) 7-9.

[16] Nichol, 28.

[17] Vinson Synan, *The Holiness-Pentecostal Movement*

in the United States (Grand Rapids: Eerdmans, 1971) 101.

[18] Nichol, 31.

STUDY GUIDE
Study Lesson 8

Of what value to 21st-century believers is the study of Pentecostal experiences in previous centuries? This section provides an interesting perspective of two individuals separated by time and geography who come to the same conclusion about tongues as the initial evidence of Spirit baptism. Please note as you study, there are no ties between Edward Irving and Charles Fox Parham. The former dies in England before the latter is born in the United States. Plus, Parham has no access to materials published by Irving.

Of further importance is the reality of Spirit baptism not being limited to only English-speaking communities within the United States. This has often been overlooked until more recent research.

SCRIPTURES

Joel 2:28, 29 has been used in a previous chapter; however, refresh your memory by reading it again and listing the specific people upon whom the Holy Spirit will come.

_____

_____

_____

_____

_____

_____

QUESTIONS AND READINGS

Read the pages that are assigned for this lesson and answer the following questions.

1. What are two distinctives of the Irvingites?

2. Why was there such a long time period between Edward's completing his education and taking his first pastorate?

3. Which two events impacted Irving's desire for spiritual gifts?

4. How did Irving's not personally experiencing Spirit baptism impact him?

5. What was the beginning emphasis or activity that led to the Shearer Schoolhouse revival?

6. How is Joel 2:28, 29 fulfilled (or seen) in the Shearer Schoolhouse revival?

7. How widespread was Spirit baptism prior to the Azusa Street Revival of 1906?

8. What were two beliefs Parham held about tongues (one is false)?

9. When did the first of Parham's students receive Spirit baptism with the evidence of tongues?

PERSONAL PERSPECTIVE

Having completed the two study lessons on chapters 7 and 8, what are some of your personal thoughts after completing the initial historical review?

Azusa to the Present

The 20th and 21st centuries provide a different picture of tongues than the previous 1,800 years. Instead of a few smaller groups on the fringe of Christianity with the distinctive of tongues and other spiritual manifestations, a number of Pentecostal denominations developed who practiced tongues-speaking. Crossing nations and continents, their numbers and influence have grown until the Pentecostal Movement has become known as the "third force" in Christianity.

Like their predecessors, these early pioneers of the Pentecostal faith experienced disdain and direct opposition from their neighbors and communities. Often seen as social outcasts because of their lower economic and educational levels, they became the objects of ridicule and physical persecution. With faithful perseverance and God's blessings, however, the scene changed. Primitive brush arbors and storefront worship facilities gave way to brick structures with padded pews and baptisteries on the "right side of the tracks." Simultaneously, many Pentecostal believers advanced economically and educationally.

The distinctive of the first half of the 20th century was the doctrinal commitment to tongues as the initial evidence of the Baptism with the Holy Spirit. With the rise of the Charismatic Movement, however, different signs or evidences of Spirit baptism were promoted as proof of the experience or filling.

Let's return to the first decade of the 1900s and trace the pattern of belief concerning tongues and Spirit baptism in the past century.

AZUSA STREET REVIVAL

There is no doubt that the Azusa Street Revival of 1906-1909 was the catalytic event that exposed and exploded Pentecostal practice and doctrine. From the humble setting of a combination tenement house and livery stable, news of the supernatural events of Spirit baptism with the evidence of tongues flowed nationally and internationally. Crowds of people came, many from great distances, to see and to experience this marvelous blessing. Then they returned home to spread the faith.

Although the story of this marvelous revival in Los Angeles is recounted in many books and articles, some of its aspects are, of necessity, included here. Besides being a vital part of Pentecostal history, our belief in tongues as the initial evidence of the baptism in the Holy Spirit speaks strongly of conditions in which true spiritual renewal occurs.

Two distinct aspects of this revival will be examined briefly. The most commonly known and referred-to event is the arrival of William J. Seymour in Los Angeles and his preaching the Pentecostal doctrine he had learned from Charles Fox Parham in Houston. The lesser-known aspect of the story is the spiritual preparation that took place for at least a year, as people sought a spiritual renewal such as was being experienced in Wales.

We begin with the spiritual preparation, as described in the writings of Frank Bartleman, an eyewitness and active participant in the revival. The marvelous revival did not take place in a spiritual vacuum. Rather, individuals were praying and desiring a spiritual renewal like what was occurring in Wales. Pastor Joseph Smale traveled to Wales, witnessed the revival events and was in touch with Evan Roberts, the leading revivalist. On his return, Smale expressed the desire "to have the same visitation and blessing come to his own church in Los Angeles."[1] Later, in the summer of 1905, Smale resigned as pastor when church officials tired of 15 weeks of daily meetings.

With individuals who desired spiritual renewal, he eventually organized a New Testament church.

Besides Smale's visit to Wales, other ties furthered the spiritual environment. G. Campbell Morgan's tract, "Revival in Wales," was widely distributed. Bartleman began selling S.B. Shaw's book, *The Great Revival in Wales*.[2] He too wrote to Evan Roberts, asking for prayer. Roberts responded. The last two lines of a Roberts' letter to Bartleman, dated November 4, 1905, read: "I pray God to hear your prayer, to keep your faith strong, and to save California. I remain, your brother in the fight."[3]

The desire for revival continued when William G. Seymour accepted the invitation to go to Los Angeles as associate pastor of the Nazarene Mission on Santa Fe Avenue. Terry Neeley, a member of the congregation, initiated this contact after meeting Seymour and receiving the baptism of the Holy Spirit in Houston, Texas.[4] The black Holiness preacher's intense desire to learn convinced Parham to permit him to sit in the hall outside the classroom where he was teaching. ("Jim Crow" laws of that era did not allow blacks and whites to be taught together.) Despite this obstacle, Seymour heard and accepted the doctrine of tongues as the initial evidence of Spirit baptism.

On arriving in Los Angeles and being given his first opportunity to preach at the church, Seymour spoke from Acts 2:4, expounding on tongues as the sign of the Baptism in the Holy Spirit. This did not agree with the doctrinal belief of Holiness people of that day, so he found himself locked out of the church. He continued his ministry, however, when he accepted the invitation of Richard and Ruth Asbury to hold services in their home.

On April 9, 1906, seven individuals, including Seymour, shared in the experience of Spirit baptism with the initial evidence of speaking in tongues.

The news of this event spread. Crowds increased at the home. Finally, it became necessary to move to another location—312 Azusa Street. Skeptics, mockers and seekers alike began coming to see what was taking place. These services continued daily for three years. Individuals, like G.B. Cashwell, traveled across the United States to attend the revival. They then returned home to begin a Pentecostal revival in their home areas. Others, wanting to visit Los Angeles but couldn't, received the baptism in the Holy Spirit in various locations in the United States.

DENOMINATIONAL IMPACT

Tongues as the initial evidence of the baptism in the Holy Spirit stands as a doctrinal distinctive of

the Azusa Street Revival. Individuals leaving Los
Angeles took this concept with them as they
returned to their home areas and churches. As
growing numbers of ministers and members of the
Holiness groups were baptized in the Holy Spirit,
these denominations faced a major decision. Would
they accept or reject this new Pentecostal doctrine
and experience? Central to their decision was the
position the leader(s) assumed.

Leaders of the Holiness denominations found
themselves in a precarious position. On one hand
they understood their responsibility for doctrinal
truth. On the other hand, they were faced with the
reality of what ministers and laity alike were experiencing. This was especially true in the Holiness
Church in North Carolina and in the Fire-
Baptized Holiness Church. Ministers and laity
from these denominations attended a revival in
Dunn, North Carolina, and many of the leaders
experienced the baptism in the Holy Spirit with
the initial sign/evidence of tongues.

J.H. King, the leader of the Fire-Baptized
Holiness Church, first began preparing to debate
the issue of tongues. In preparing, however, he
convinced himself of its validity, and personally
received the experience on February 15, 1907. His
contemporary in the Holiness Church, A.B.
Crumpler, not only rejected tongues but returned
to the Methodist church.

A.J. Tomlinson was in a different situation, since some of the members in the Church of God had received the Spirit baptism in the Shearer Schoolhouse Revival in 1896. Also, he had preached the reality of the experience for nearly a year before personally receiving the baptism in the Holy Spirit.

A divisive situation arose in the Church of God in Christ as the cofounders disagreed on the subject. C.P. Jones rejected the Pentecostal view and C.H. Mason accepted it. In an unusual series of events, Jones had Mason disfellowshiped. He then changed the name of his organization to "The Church of Christ (Holiness) U.S.A." This allowed Mason and those who accepted the Pentecostal view to use the name "Church of God in Christ."

The view adopted by A.B. Simpson and the Christian and Missionary Alliance was different than any of the others. After a great deal of investigation, Simpson decided to reject the Pentecostal view. Simpson had earlier anticipated an outpouring of the Holy Spirit that would include manifestation such as tongues, miracles and prophecy. His rejection of tongues as initial evidence included the charge that it spawned "a preoccupation with spiritual manifestations rather than cultivating a devotion to God, and tended to reduce evangelistic zeal."[5]

Since many within the denomination had received the Spirit baptism with tongues, a conflict occurred. Many members left. Some, however, chose to remain and provide leadership for the denomination. This resulted in an Alliance where even today, some are of the "Holiness Movement" and others of the "Pentecostal persuasion."

Two other denominations differed from those already mentioned. Neither were in existence before the Azusa Street Revival. Florence Crawford received the baptism in the Holy Spirit in the early months of the Azusa revival, and moved to Portland, Oregon. There, she began The Apostolic Faith Church in 1907. Self-described as Trinitarian, fundamental and evangelistic, this denomination initiated "cutting edge" methods of outreach in its earlier decades—a move that distinguished it from other Pentecostal groups of the era.[6] They held firmly to tongues as the initial evidence of Spirit baptism. Although still in existence, the group unfortunately plateaued and has experienced considerable decline.

The Assemblies of God formed as a loosely knit organization five years after the Azusa revival. Congregations under this Pentecostal umbrella came from white congregations with ties to the Church of God in Christ and from independent congregations that developed from the spread of the

Pentecostal experience. One of the distinctive doctrines of the group is evidential tongues. Although a few questioned this position, the denominational leadership took a strong doctrinal stand on tongues as the initial evidence of Spirit baptism.

CHARISMATIC MOVEMENT

The middle of the 20th century occasioned a new move of the Spirit, known as Neo-Pentecostalism, or the Charismatic Movement. In a 1975 summary, J. Rodman Williams offered this profile of the movement's emergence:

> The Charismatic Movement began with the historic churches in the 1950s. On the American scene it started to attract broad attention in 1960 with the national publicity given to the ministry of the Reverend Dennis Bennett, an Episcopalian in Van Nuys, California. Since then there has been a continuing growth within many of the mainline churches: first, such Protestant churches as Episcopal, Lutheran and Presbyterian; second, the Roman Catholic (beginning in 1967); and third, the Greek Orthodox (beginning about 1971).[7]

This renewal, like other spiritual revivals, came through a sovereign move of God. During the 1940s and 1950s, many people in mainline Protestant denominations received the baptism in the Holy Spirit. Slowly, the news of this phenomenon reached the Pentecostal churches. Several factors influenced this wave of renewal and emphasis on the Holy Spirit.

One factor was the ministry of the various healing revivalists from about 1947 to about 1958. Nearly every healing revivalist was a practicing Pentecostal. People perceived these men as healers as well as preachers of salvation. Yet, the emphasis on healing and other miracles drew people into a new dimension of understanding about the ministry of the Holy Spirit. Without speaking directly on either the need or opportunity for Spirit baptism, people were led to hunger and desire for the work of the Spirit in their lives.

Another factor is the founding and ministry of the Full Gospel Business Men's Fellowship International (FGBMFI). Through the vision, leadership and financial support of Demos Shakarian, a wealthy dairy farmer, FGBMFI reached out to businessmen, sharing their faith in Christ and the joy of the Holy Spirit. The impact of this organization can be measured partially by its growth and expansion. From its founding in October 1951 with 21 men until 1972, over 1,100 chapters were founded in 52 countries.

One person who figures in both of these areas is Oral Roberts. Not only was he a leading healing revivalist, but he also played a part in the founding of the FGBMFI. Roberts encouraged Shakarian's vision for the organization, and was the guest speaker at its first meeting in Los Angeles.

No review of the Charismatic Movement would be complete without noting several of the leading individuals from various denominations. Their experiences, preaching/teaching, publications and organizational activities furthered this spiritual renewal with emphasis on the ministry of the Holy Spirit.

Dennis Bennett was one of the early voices of Charismatic renewal for Episcopalians, Lutherans and Presbyterians. Serving as rector of St. Mark's Episcopalian Church in Van Nuys, California, he received the baptism in the Holy Spirit and spoke in tongues in November 1959. He felt obligated to share accounts of this experience with his church, and several months later a negative fervor developed in the congregation that necessitated his resignation. Word of the Charismatic events at St. Mark's became national news, however, through coverage by both *Newsweek* and *Time* magazines.

From a new base of ministry at a revitalized St. Luke's Episcopal Church in Seattle, Bennett traveled throughout the United States and other countries, sharing his testimony of how God led him to

the fullness of the Holy Spirit. He shared this testimony in such an inviting manner that individuals whose hearts and minds were touched and
intrigued would come at the end of the meetings
to hear the "rest of the story."

Three years after the death of his first wife,
Elberta, Bennett married Rita Marie Reed. Together
they ministered in conferences and co-authored
several books, including *The Holy Spirit*, which
stated their doctrine of the Holy Spirit and became
a best seller.

Although they were not in the first small group of
Roman Catholics to receive the Holy Spirit with
speaking in tongues, Kevin and Dorothy Ranaghan
soon rose to the forefront of the movement's leadership. Both of them were theology professors at the
University of Notre Dame. They heard that their
friends at Duquesne University in Pittsburg were
seeking the Pentecostal experience. This created dif-
ficulty for them because they did not understand
the actions of their fellow theology instructors. One
of these friends, Ralph Keifer, spent several days in
South Bend, answering all their possible objections.

Less than a month later, on March 5, 1967, the
Ranaghans and seven friends met in an apart-
ment, with a firm determination to pursue the
baptism in the Holy Spirit. Laying hands on each
other, they prayed to "be filled with the gifts and
the fruit of the Holy Spirit, that our lives might be
more fully Christian."[8]

There was no prophecy, no speaking in tongues. There was, however, a newness in prayer, a newness that for many of us marked the beginning of a deeper faith life. We had sought in Jesus' name the fullness of the life of the Holy Spirit, and within us the change had begun.[9]

The Ranaghans were prominent leaders in the Catholic Charismatic renewal. Their activities were focused on planning and organizing major Charismatic conferences for Catholics, speaking at conferences, teaching and writing. Their book, *Catholic Pentecostals*, released in 1969, shares events and testimonies of the renewal within Catholicism.

In the Lutheran Church, Laurence (Larry) Christianson is another leader within the Charismatic Movement. A Minnesota native, he graduated in 1959 from Luther Theological Seminary in St. Paul. He became the pastor of the Trinity Lutheran Church in San Pedro, California; and in 1961, Christianson received the baptism in the Holy Spirit with the experience of speaking in tongues. He proceeded to lead his congregation in a revival of Pentecost.

Christianson's influence spread far beyond the United States. In 1963, he led two Anglican curates into the Pentecostal experience, marking a special impact of the Charismatic Movement in the British Isles. His booklet, *Speaking in Tongues: A Gift for the*

Body of Christ, was published in London. It was also translated into German and received extended circulation.[10]

DOCTRINAL DIFFERENCE

Although the Pentecostal and Charismatic Movements share a common tie in their emphasis on the baptism in the Holy Spirit and spiritual gifts, certain defined differences cannot be overlooked. The terms are not synonymous. The most evident for our consideration is the issue of tongues as the evidence/sign of Spirit baptism. Pentecostal denominations hold to a clearly stated doctrine of tongues being the outward, physical sign of having received the baptism in the Holy Spirit. Here are some quotes from their doctrinal statements or position papers.

Apostolic Faith (Portland, Oregon)

> The BAPTISM OF THE HOLY GHOST is the enduement of power from on high upon the clean, sanctified life and is evidenced by speaking in tongues as the Spirit gives the utterance (Luke 24:49; Acts 1:5-8; 2:1-4).[11]

Assemblies of God

Baptism in the Holy Spirit is the specific event that introduces the believer to the ongoing process of living a Spirit-empowered life. Although speaking in tongues is the outward sign of Spirit baptism, it is designed by God to be much more than evidence. . . . The expression *initial physical evidence of the baptism of the Holy Spirit* refers to the first outward, observable sign that the Holy Spirit has come in filling power. . . . There is no statement or implication of a delay between the event of the baptism in the Spirit and the evidence of speaking in tongues.[12]

Church of God

Article 9 of the Declaration of Faith states:

We believe "in speaking with other tongues as the Spirit gives utterance and that it is the initial evidence of the baptism in the Holy Ghost."[13]

Church of God in Christ

When one receives a baptismal Holy Ghost experience, we believe one will speak with a tongue unknown to oneself according to the sovereign will of God.[14]

Church of God of Prophecy

Speaking in tongues is the evidence of the baptism of the Holy Ghost (Acts 2:4; 10:44-46; 19:6; 1 Corinthians 12:10, 11; 14:2, 4, 15).[15]

Congregational Holiness Church, Inc.

We believe in the baptism with the Holy Ghost, and speaking with other tongues, as the Spirit gives utterance to be the initiatory evidence of this experience (Acts 2:4; 10:44-46; 19:6).[16]

Pentecostal Church of God

The Baptism of the Holy Ghost is accompanied with the speaking in other tongues as the Holy Spirit Himself gives utterance, as the initial physical sign and evidence (Acts 2:4).[17]

In contrast, within the Charismatic Movement, there is no clearly defined doctrine of an evidence or sign of Spirit baptism. A plethora of views exists, ranging from tongues as the definite evidence of Spirit baptism to viewing one of the gifts of the Spirit or a virtue of the fruit of the Spirit being the evidence.

Several quotes from the Bennett's book, *The Holy Spirit and You*, indicates a belief in a distinct sign:

> "It comes with the package!" Speaking in tongues is not the baptism in the Holy Spirit, but it is what happens when and as you are baptized in the Spirit and it becomes an important resource to help you continue . . .[18]
>
> You don't have to speak in tongues to have times of feeling filled with the Holy Spirit, but

if you want the free and full outpouring that
is the baptism of the Holy Spirit, you must
expect it to happen as in the Scriptures.[19]

On the opposite side of the spectrum are the
testimonies of individuals who claim Spirit baptism due to having a new sense of joy, faith and
love apart from ever speaking in tongues. The
Ranaghans include many of these early testimonies.[20] As we read them, however, it appears
these people are experiencing the fullness of salvation in a manner previously unknown.

This corresponds with what my father, the
Reverend John Daffe, stated after hearing the testimony of a Roman Catholic priest who spoke of
having received the baptism in the early 1960s. To
the best of my recollection, his words were, "Son,
it sounds like he has a good case of salvation."

Some years later Dr. Sherwood Wirt, editor
emeritus of *Decision* magazine, visited the campus
of Northwest Bible College and shared how he
knew he had received the baptism in the Holy
Spirit. He said that a cantankerous Presbyterian
minister now loves people. Many of us sitting in
that circle thought of that experience as either salvation or sanctification.

This lack of a distinct evidence/sign of Spirit
baptism can be seen readily in the doctrinal statements of Charismatic denominations and fellow-
ships. They emphasize the work of the Holy Spirit

in varied dimensions, but without any commitment to a specific sign of the baptism in the Holy Spirit. *The Vineyard* Statement of Faith provides an excellent example:

> We believe in the filling or empowerment of the Holy Spirit, often a conscious experience, for ministry today. We believe in the present ministry of the Spirit and in the exercise of all of the Biblical gifts of the Spirit. We practice the laying on of hands for the empowering of the Spirit, for healing, and for recognition and empowering of those whom God has ordained to lead and to serve the Church.[21]

Before leaving the section, it should be noted that the concept of no distinct evidence or sign isn't original to the Charismatic Movement. R.A. Torrey, American evangelist and Biblical scholar as well as the first superintendent of Moody Bible Institute (1889-1908), provides a prime example. In 1927 a series of his addresses on the Holy Spirit were published in a book titled *The Holy Spirit*. These three quotes provide a bird's-eye view of his position on Spirit baptism:

> In the first place, the Baptism with the Holy Spirit is a definite experience of which one may know whether he has received it or not. This is clear from Acts 1:4, 5. . . . It is clear as

a day from these verses that the Baptism with the Holy Ghost is a definite experience of which a man may know whether he has received it or not, for if not, how could the disciples possibly know when the days of waiting were over and the days to begin their ministry had begun?[22]

Later in the same chapter, Torrey writes:

And I wondered if everyone who was baptized with the Holy Spirit would not speak with tongues. And as I did not see anyone speaking with tongues today, I wondered if this gift was not confined to the Apostolic age. . . . So I saw that the teaching, speaking with tongues, was the inevitable and invariable result of being baptized with the Holy Spirit, and that any one who had not spoken with tongues had not been baptized with the Holy Spirit, was utterly unscriptural and anti-scriptural.[23]

Torrey strongly believed in the need to be Spirit-baptized, however:

In light of all these facts, we are abundantly warranted in saying that every child of God is under the most solemn obligation to see to it that he definitely receives the Holy Spirit, not merely as a regenerating power and as an indwelling presence, but as a definite enduement with power, before he undertakes service of any kind for God.[24]

At this point, the question arises: "Does it really matter what we believe about initial evidence, as long as a person strives to live holy and be Spirit-led?" We respond with a strong "Yes, it does!" There are issues that are a part of the greater whole to this doctrinal perspective. The ongoing challenge for each of us, as believers, is to carefully consider the whole picture and not become trapped or entangled with a narrow perspective that does not allow the fullness of the Holy Spirit to be evident in our lives.

ENDNOTES

¹ Frank Bartleman, *Azusa Street* (Plainfield, NJ: Logos, 1980) 13.

² Bartleman, 11.

³ Bartleman, 13.

⁴ John Thomas Nichol, *Pentecostalism,* (New York: Harper and Row, 1966) 33.

⁵ Charles Nienkirchen, "Simpson, Albert Benjamin," in *Dictionary of Pentecostal and Charismatic Movements,* ed. Stanley M. Burgess and Gary B. MeGee (Grand Rapids: Regency Reference Library, 1988) 786.

⁶ For further information, read *A Historical Account of the Apostolic Faith.* This book is a compilation by veteran members of the organization. It was published in 1965.

⁷ J. Rodman Williams, "A Profile of the Charismatic Movement," *Christianity Today,* Feb. 28, 1975: 9.

⁸ Kevin and Dorothy Ranaghan, *Catholic Pentecostals* (New York: Paulist, 1969) 40.

⁹ Ranaghan, 40.

¹⁰ Richard Quebedeaux, *The New Charismatics Origin, Development and Significance of Neo-Pentecostalism* (Garden City, KS: Doubleday, 1976) 60.

¹¹ The Apostolic Faith Church, "Bible Doctrines," Online <http://www.apostolicfaith.org/aboutus /doctrinal.asp> Retrieved Oct. 25, 2004.

[12] These statements are taken from "The Baptism in the Holy Spirit: The Initial Experience and Continuing Evidence of the Spirit-Filled Life," a position paper adopted by the General Presbytery of the General Council of the Assemblies of God, Aug. 11, 2000. Online <http://ag.org/top/beliefs/position-papers/4185-spirit-filled-life.cfm> Retrieved July 7, 2004.

[13] This position is repeated in the Doctrinal Commitments section of the *Supplement to the Minutes* with the following Scripture references: John 15:26; Acts 2:4, 10:44-46; 19:1-7.

[14] "The Doctrines of the Church of God in Christ," Online <http://www.cogic.org/dctrn.htm>.

[15] Church of God of Prophecy "Important Bible Truths," Online *<http:// worldwide.cogop.org/index.php?module=contentepress&func=display&ceid=18>* Retrieved Oct. 26, 2004.

[16] Congregational Holiness Church, Inc., "Articles of Faith," Online *<http://www.chchurch.com/What_We_Believe.html>* Retrieved Oct. 25, 2004.

[17] "Our Beliefs." The denominational position is taken from the Web site of a local Pentecostal Church of God congregation. Online *<http://www.lafpcg.org/belief.html>* Retrieved Oct. 25, 2004.

[18] Dennis and Rita Bennett, *The Holy Spirit and You* (Plainfield, NJ.: Logos International, 1971) 64.

[19] Bennett, 65.

[20] Ranaghan, 58-106.

[21] Bill Jackson, *The Quest for the Radical Middle: A History of the Vineyard* (Cape Town, South Africa: Vineyard International, 1999) 411.

[22] R.A. Torrey, *The Holy Spirit* (Grand Rapids: Fleming H. Revell, 1927) 107.

[23] Torrey, 128.

[24] Torrey, 140.

STUDY GUIDE
Study Lesson 9

What is the doctrinal position on the baptism of the Holy Spirit held by your local church and/or denomination? (Write a short statement of what you believe it to be.)

Check on the accuracy of your statement by reviewing either your local church's or denomination's doctrinal statement of faith.

HISTORICAL PERSPECTIVE

This chapter begins with a brief review of the Azusa Street Revival, which becomes the catalyst for the rise of independent Pentecostal congregations and many Holiness denominations becoming Pentecostal. It continues with an overview of the rise of the Charismatic Movement. Also included are the doctrinal statements of various denominations, which partially reflect the differences between a Pentecostal and Charismatic perspective.

QUESTIONS AND READINGS

1. Who are the following individuals? Write a one-sentence definition.

    William J. Seymour

    Joseph Smale

Frank Bartleman

J.H. King

A.B. Simpson

Florence Crawford

Demos Shakarian

Dennis Bennett

Kevin and Dorothy Ranaghan

Larry Christensen

R.A. Torrey

2. What is the difference between Pentecostals and Charismatics that is most evident?

PERSONAL PERSPECTIVE

Take a few moments and consider the factors (people, events, ideas) that have influenced your current view of the baptism in the Holy Spirit. Write them down to be considered later after having completed this study.

Part IV

Reappearing
Issues

Persistent Concerns

I n discussing whether tongues is the initial evidence of Spirit baptism, several issues surface regularly. Their commonality by no means detracts from their importance. Often, it seems the opposite is true. These vital issues deserve our careful consideration. Too frequently we meet individuals with belief structures that are built on faulty foundations. These people, who should be a valued resource, rely instead on reasoning that ranges from "it sounds good to me," all the way to the standard response of "this is what someone else has said." All of us must take the time to carefully review and evaluate the Scriptures and philosophies which impact our views.

This chapter focuses on five recurring discussions in the dialogue on tongues as the initial evidence of the baptism in the Holy Spirit. We hold no animosity with those who hold a different position. Anyone who is in Christ, regardless of denomination or position, is our brother or sister. At the same time, we have an obligation to press for careful review of the foundations of belief.

CAN DOCTRINE BE DRAWN FROM NARRATIVE?

The argument that doctrine cannot be drawn from narrative is really an outdated one, but it continues to surface. It is outdated because modern scholarship has reaffirmed the importance and power of narrative.

"Most Biblical scholars today agree that Biblical narratives express the theological views of their authors. This used to be a point of contention between classical Pentecostals, who claimed narrative could teach theology and could therefore be used as a base for doctrine, and many non-Pentecostals who claimed it could not."[1]

In his preface to Roger Stronstad's *The Charismatic Theology of St. Luke*, Clark Pinnock stated, "Nor have we any right, as the custom is among Evangelicals, to put Luke down because his work is narrative and not didactic theology. Stronstad clears up these confusions, as well as others, and gives us here a solid basis for Pentecostal thinking and practice."[2]

"Today, this approach is known as narrative theology, in which storytelling is used to teach doctrine. Indeed, storytelling is a widely used technique in Scripture, including Luke/Acts. Deriving normative doctrine and practice from narratives is a valid exercise."[3]

Jesus himself used storytelling to communicate truths. The parables are great examples of Jesus' storytelling. After telling some of the parables, Jesus helped the disciples to understand their meaning, but He did not explain every one of them. Does this mean that the truths from the ones not elaborated on are invalid for teaching? If Jesus had not intended truth to be drawn from these parables, He would not have told them.

The "story" is safe enough for others to enter, and powerful enough to engage them and potentially change them. The story is to be experienced; and the person is expected to learn and to be changed by the experience. Luke was not interested in merely reporting history; he wanted the people of God to know the certainty of the teaching and to experience Holy Spirit fullness so they could continue the work of Jesus.

Recent years have seen a recovery of storytelling. In the 21st century, "story" is used in teaching and preaching as the vehicle through which theological truths are communicated.

"All Scripture is given by inspiration of God,
and is profitable for doctrine, for reproof,
for correction, for instruction in righteousness, that the man of God may be complete,
thoroughly equipped for every good work"
(2 Timothy 3:16, 17).

Paul further affirmed, "For whatever was written in former days was written for our instruction"
(Romans 15:4, *NRSV*). "If for Paul the historical
narratives of the Old Testament had didactic lessons for New Testament Christians, then it would
be most surprising if Luke, who modeled his historiography after the Old Testament historiography,
did not invest his own history of the origin and
spread of Christianity with a didactic significance."[4]

The point is that recent Biblical scholarship has
demonstrated the validity of narrative theology. The
challenge is to exercise appropriate exegetical skills
in interpreting the various forms of literature. May
God grant His superintending and illumination.

SPIRITUAL GIFTS: 1 Corinthians 12

How marvelous it is that through the work of
the Holy Spirit in the lives of believers, the church,
corporate and local, can be equipped to minister!
This equipping through spiritual gifts enables a
person to accomplish what is not possible within
the parameters of individual abilities and talents.

It is important for us to understand that spiritual gifts are not an enhancement of natural virtue that comes from one's gene pool. Rather, spiritual gifts are specific abilities divinely granted by choice of the Holy Spirit. It is equally important to understand that a spiritual gift isn't the evidence of Spirit baptism.

We focus on 1 Corinthians 12 because a portion of verse 30 frequently appears in the presentation of those who say tongues are not the initial evidence of Spirit baptism: "Do all speak in tongues?" (*NIV*). Left to itself or plucked out of context, this question raises what appears to be a legitimate position. Proper Biblical interpretation and understanding always depend on considering the context of the question, however.

In chapter 12, the apostle Paul deals with two distinct topics—spiritual gifts and the unity of the body within the church. Nowhere in this chapter, or in the following two chapters where tongues are mentioned again, do we find any hint or direct reference to the experience of Spirit baptism. The overriding issue is spiritual gifts and their operation within the local church. These believers had already experienced the baptism in the Holy Spirit and had spoken in tongues. Paul wrote to help them understand the continuing operation of the Spirit in their corporate lives.

The chapter begins with an express statement of purpose. He doesn't want them "to be ignorant" of spiritual gifts. Notice the absence of any reference to Spirit baptism. Surely if this were the topic, it would be so indicated. The apostle Paul isn't known for "beating around the bush" about any subject. Tactful? Yes. Hidden references? No. A good example is Paul's approach to the disciples in Ephesus (Acts 19). He got right to the point: "Did you receive the Holy Spirit . . . ?" (v. 2).

In the same way, Paul stays on target in 1 Corinthians 12. He wants them to know that spiritual gifts are available, and they complement each other. Each gift is valuable, though some are more public and sensational than others. To demonstrate, he uses the wonderful analogy of the human body. Some parts are evident while others are modestly hidden; yet, each serves a vital part in the proper functioning of the body.

No one is ever given a nonessential spiritual gift! Each person's gift continues to be vital to the functioning of the church as a whole, as well as to us individually. "Now to each one the manifestation of the Spirit is given for the common good" (v. 7, *NIV*).

This chapter points directly to the means by which believers receive spiritual gifts. The Holy Spirit determines, or chooses, which gift (or gifts) are to be operative in our lives (v. 11). We can desire or ask for other spiritual gifts to become evident within us (v. 31), but whether we receive it (them) depends on the Sovereign will. He knows what is truly best for us . . . and what the church needs. Of special interest is the lack of an indication of a point in time or an event when these gifts are received.

As Paul continues to show the importance, yet distinction, of God's choice and will for believers, he asks a series of questions in verses 29 and 30. This is a continuation and further emphasis of what he previously stated in the chapter. God, through the Holy Spirit, calls individuals to different positions in the body of Christ. Through the ministry of the Holy Spirit, believers receive different spiritual gifts.

So we return to the original position. Nowhere in any of these verses does the apostle mention Spirit baptism or any of these gifts being evidence of that event in their lives.

One last look at content includes chapter 14. Here the apostle offers guidelines for the ministry of spiritual gifts in a worship service. Verse 12 is important: "Since you are eager to have spiritual gifts, try to excel in gifts that build up the church" (NIV). It seems logical to ask this question: *If spiritual gifts can be evidence of Spirit baptism, why didn't Paul remind them of this major spiritual event?*

Before leaving this segment, one other item needs clarification. The baptism in the Holy Spirit *is* a gift from God to believers. It is not in the same category as spiritual gifts, however. The baptism in the Holy Spirit provides empowerment for the individual believer; spiritual gifts provide edification for the body that enables the church to fulfill its identity and purpose in the world.

ONE LORD, ONE FAITH, ONE BAPTISM

Some use "one Lord, one faith, one baptism" to signify that the Christian experiences everything needed at conversion. Note the Scriptural context of this verse: "There is one body and one Spirit, just as you were called in one hope of your calling; one Lord, one faith, one baptism; one God and Father of all, who is above all, and through all, and in you all" (Ephesians 4:4-6). Paul is discussing the unique unity that believers have in the body of Christ.

Further, how Paul uses *baptism* must be understood. He is speaking of being "baptized" (incorporated into or immersed into) the body of Christ. In Galatians 3:27, Paul said, "For as many of you as were baptized into Christ have put on Christ." Paul also addressed this same concern in 1 Corinthians 12:13, "For by one Spirit we were all baptized into one body." The Holy Spirit baptizes the repentant person into the body of Christ.

Luke used the term, *baptized in the Holy Spirit*, (Acts 1:5; 11:16) to refer to the promise that Jesus gave concerning power to witness and fulfill mission (Luke 24:49). In Paul's reference, the Holy Spirit is the administrator, and Christ or Christ's body is the element into which the repentant person is baptized.

In John's baptism, John is the administrator and water is the element. In the promised baptism of power, Jesus is the administrator and the Holy Spirit is the element into which the believer is baptized. Paul, (the writer of Ephesians 4:4-6; 1 Corinthians 12:13; and Galatians 3:27) had been converted or baptized into Christ on the road to Damascus. Three days later, Paul was baptized in the Holy Spirit.

There is only one baptism into the Body, and this is what the Book of Ephesians addresses. The baptism into the Body is then testified to in water baptism. The baptism in the Holy Spirit, then, directs and empowers the believer for ministry.

SOULWINNING AND SPIRIT BAPTISM

How can someone be a successful evangelist, winning many people to Christ, and not have experienced the baptism in the Holy Spirit? Initially, this may appear to be a legitimate question when looking at some of the more dominant evangelists in the past several centuries who do not claim to have spoken in tongues. Indeed they believed they had experienced the baptism in the Holy Spirit, or a mighty move of the Spirit.

Charles Finney records what he called "receiving the baptism of the Holy Ghost." His first experience occurs on the evening of the day of his conversion, October 10, 1821:

> But as I turned and was about to take a seat by the fire, I received a mighty baptism of the Holy Ghost. Without any expectation of it, without any recollection that I had ever heard the thing mentioned by any person in the world, the Holy Spirit descended upon me in a manner that seemed to go through me, body and soul. I could feel the impression, like a wave of electricity, going through and through me. Indeed, it seemed to come in waves and waves of liquid love; for I could not express it in any other way.
>
> I wept aloud with joy and love; and I did not know what I should say, I literally bellowed out the unutterable gushings of my heart. These waves came over me, and over me, one after the other, until I recollect I cried out, "I shall die if these waves continue to pass over me."[5]

In later years Finney experienced several encounters with the Holy Spirit (1834, 1838, and 1843). He
then began to teach Spirit baptism as distinct from
re-birth, as a means of keeping believers from
becoming lukewarm and as the means for full erad-
ication of sin.[6]

Being unable to return to the actual time and personally view what takes place is a disadvantage for
us. We cannot assume what the record does not
allow. We know, however, that Finney had a dramatic encounter with the Divine. This experience is
possible for all who pointedly place themselves at
the disposal of the Lord for service.

When you read the rest of the story, you find
Finney to be this kind of person. On the day of his
conversion, he quit work as a lawyer and went on
the Lord's retainer. His evangelistic fervor and
method enabled many to find Christ, even when
Finney erroneously believed a person could make
a decision for Christ without conviction of sin.
Later, he understood that this is not true.

D.L. Moody is another example. Although poorly
educated, this energetic man rose to international
fame as an evangelist. He never claimed to be anyone special. He even refused denominational cre-
dentials because of his lack of theological education, and preferred to be known as Mr. Moody. He
knew that wherever he went, there were better

preachers. He credited his success to the Lord's choosing to use him.

Early in his ministry Moody attempted to be effective through energetic work. His lack of Bible study soon revealed itself in pointless preaching, however. There were some conversions, but his ministry was severely anemic. Two women began to pray for him to receive the power of the Spirit. Initially, he resisted the very thought. Several months later Moody invited them to join him in prayer every Friday afternoon.

Months passed. Moody agonized even to the point of rolling on the floor with tears and groaning. Sometime later, while in New York City, Moody surrendered his will to God and personally experienced a mighty move of the Holy Spirit. "I can only say that God revealed Himself to me, and I had such an experience of His love that I had to ask Him to stay His hand."[7] After this experience, Moody went into full-time evangelism and experienced fame on both sides of the Atlantic Ocean.

Once again we see a setting in which God used a person who became open to His will and did not rely on personal choice or ability. In the cases of both Finney and Moody, the issue isn't Spirit baptism. First and foremost is their willingness to surrender to God's call and then stay focused to accomplish it with His help.

Spirit baptism is not a prerequisite for soulwinning. Keep in mind that as soon as we accept Jesus Christ as Savior, the Holy Spirit begins His residence with us. This is part of the salvation package. As we yield to His direction, we are able to successfully share the news of Jesus and offer His salvation to unbelievers. Some individuals are called to win souls in a greater way than others, but this is not dependent on Spirit baptism. Ministry flows outward from any person who allows the Holy Spirit to empower his or her words and actions. Marvelous aspects of ministry develop for all who work to fulfill God's calling and seek His direction and strength!

There is power in relationship with God. Consider the account of the 12 disciples being sent out to minister (Matthew 10). Jesus directed them to preach and perform miracles of healing, raising the dead and casting out demons. Keep in mind that this was several years prior to their receiving the baptism in the Holy Spirit on the Day of Pentecost (Acts 2).

Not to be overlooked is the ministry of the 70 disciples. As Jesus sent them out to minister, He included the directive to heal the sick (Luke 10:1-16). When they returned, their joyous reports included domination over demons (v. 17). In each case, individuals were used in a powerful ministry without the distinct experiences of Spirit baptism.

YOU CANNOT PUT GOD IN A BOX

The argument, "You cannot put God in a box," is used to refute speaking in tongues as being "normative," or as being the "initial physical evidence" of the baptism in the Holy Spirit. This argument says that God is free and that you set up barriers by stating a norm or setting rules. It is true that we cannot set the rules by which God operates. We cannot force Him to work according to our design. God is sovereign—He is completely in charge. God is free.

God is free, but He is neither arbitrary nor capricious. This means that God does not operate without fixed laws, and He does not abuse others with His unlimited power. God is consistent with His character and will. He is free to set rules, establish patterns and choose the ways He will deal with human beings. God does not change His approach to confuse individuals and keep them guessing. God is consistent. Creation itself demonstrates His consistency. God is free to change the power of the sun and the influence of the moon, but He set the pattern by which they work. We do not say we are putting God, the Creator and Sustainer of the universe, in a box when we say we expect the pattern of days and nights to continue.

In relationship to "speaking in tongues," we need to try to understand God's revelation, discern His patterns and submit to His ways. By insisting that a person does not have to speak in tongues, we resist God and forfeit His gift. We might think or say that surely God can package His gifts in a more palatable way for contemporary Christians, but our thinking or speaking does not change God's approach.

Consider the consistency God has demonstrated in Scripture and in history. Acknowledge His patterns of giving assurance to individuals that they have been baptized in the Holy Spirit.

MANUAL GLOSSOLALIA

What about those individuals who are unable to speak and must use sign language to communicate? Wouldn't the view of tongues as the initial evidence of Spirit baptism be discriminatory?

These questions raise several issues for consideration. First, signed language is on the same level as verbal language. Both enable a person to communicate. The mode or method is the only difference. One uses vocal cords and sounds while the other uses hands with distinct shapes and patterns. Second, glossolalia involves speaking in a language unknown to the person. There isn't anything in the concept that determines speaking in tongues to be exclusively verbal speech.

Though there are testimonies of these occurrences dating back to the 1940s, it has only been since the

1990s that manual glossolalia has received greater recognition. In her article "Manual Glossolalia," Dr. JoAnn Smith records the experience of a retired deaf evangelist. "Our hands would take on different shapes and movements we could not recognize, but we just assumed it was all part of our enthusiastic praise."[19]

There are other instances in which a person is enabled to speak audibly in tongues at the moment of Spirit baptism. An early example can be read in the July 10, 1948, issue of *The Pentecostal Evangel*. In the process of sharing coverage of the national convention of the Christian Deaf Fellowship which met at Central Bible Institute in Springfield, Missouri (June 9-13, 1948), the experience of Kenneth Courtney is included: "One young man who plans to enter the deaf Bible School this fall, was gloriously filled with the Holy Spirit in the car just outside of Springfield en route to the convention, and arrived on the campus speaking audibly in other tongues."[20]

This isn't an isolated experience of the past. Others who are involved in deaf ministries continue to share accounts of the Holy Spirit's speaking through manual glossolalia and temporarily loosened vocal cords. Related to this are the incidents of messages in tongues being given either vocally or manually and then being interpreted by someone using sign language.

ENDNOTES

[1] Donald A. Johns, "Some New Directions in the Hermeneutics of Classical Pentecostalism's Doctrine of Initial Evidence," *Initial Evidence* Gary B. McGee, ed. (Peabody, MA: Hendrickson, 1991) 151, 152.

[2] Roger Stronstad, *The Charismatic Theology of St. Luke* (Peabody, MA: Hendrickson, 1984) vii.

[3] French Arrington, *Encountering the Holy Spirit* (Cleveland, TN: Pathway, 2003) 172.

[4] Roger Stronstad, *The Charismatic Theology of St. Luke* (Peabody, Massachusetts: Hendrickson, 1984) 7.

[5] Charles G. Finney, *Memories of Rev. Charles G. Finney*, 20, 21.

[6] Paulus Sharpff, *History of Evangelism* (Grand Rapids: Eerdman's, 1966) 108.

[7] John Pollock, *Moody: A Biographical Portrait* (Grand Rapids: Zondervan, 1967) 90.

[8] JoAnn Smith, "Manual Glossolalia," in *The New Dictionary of the Pentecostal Charismatic Movements*, ed. Stanley M. Burgess (Grand Rapids: Zondervan, 2002) 677, 678.

[9] "Great Convention of Deaf-Mutes," *The Pentecostal Evangel*, No. 1748, July 10, 1948: 11, 12.

STUDY GUIDE
Study Lesson 10

What are some positions or arguments against tongues being the initial evidence of Spirit baptism which you have heard?

Do these positions appear to be carefully thought through and Biblically based? Or do they seem to be the result of simply adopting what someone else has said?

A PERSPECTIVE

It's amazing how often well-intentioned people with the ability to think, to research and to analyze frequently take the easy route of not caring about issues or simply adopting what another person believes (parent, pastor, friend). Hopefully they can be trusted! But, when it comes to issues which have earthly and even heavenly consequences, they deserve our personal attention!

This chapter draws attention to six issues for consideration. The first five are frequently heard in discussions. The sixth is infrequent but needs to be noted in the overall consideration of speaking in tongues as the initial evidence.

STUDY QUESTIONS

1. What is narrative theology?

2. Review the section in chapter 2 which covers the five historical records of individuals receiving the distinct experience of Spirit baptism. Luke tells the stories (accounts) of what takes place, from which we develop doctrinal truths.

3. Look up 2 Timothy 3:16, 17 and write out these important verses.

4. What is the one-sentence definition of spiritual gifts?

5. After reading 1 Corinthians 12, how often does the apostle Paul mention Spirit baptism?

6. What is the difference of purpose between the baptism in the Holy Spirit and spiritual gifts?

7. Baptism into the body of Christ is signified by what event?

8. What is the foremost factor in the evangelistic success of Charles Finney and D.L. Moody?

9. True or False: Any powerful ministry flows outward from relationship with God.

10. True or False: The argument of "You can't put God in a box" overlooks the consistency of God's will and character.

11. What is manual glossolalia?

PERSPECTIVE

At this point you have read 10 chapters of *Speaking in Tongues: Initial Evidence of Spirit Baptism* and completed each of the study-guide lessons. What do you believe about the baptism in the Holy Spirit and tongues as the initial evidence, and why?

Perspective

"**I** think . . ."
"Well, the way I see it . . ."
"I believe . . ."

Without their completing the sentence, it is obvious each speaker has an opinion. At some point a decision was made about options, and the person arrived at an opinion—before it was expressed. Regardless of the subject or significance of the issue, individuals utilize perspective when they come to their positions.

We all do. Each believer faces a tremendous challenge, namely building personal beliefs on the right foundation. This process is complicated by a number of less-than-positive influences. Although all of them do not impact each of us in the same manner, they may be evident in our thinking to a greater degree than we are aware. An increase in chronological age does not automatically bring advanced immunity to these influences.

God created us with the ability to think, to analyze and to come to conclusions. This enables us to make decisions. Some decisions are insignificant, such as *Do we buy the generic brand or the name brand? Or, What should we eat for lunch?* Others have far greater significance when dealing with relationships, medical treatments and financial commitments. Of even greater importance is our perspective on spiritual beliefs and actions. What is the foundational presupposition with which we begin? This is a vital question we must answer.

PRIORITY OF SCRIPTURE

People take four basic approaches in determining truth.

The first of these is reasoning. God has given us the ability to think, to analyze, to synthesize and to draw conclusions. God wants us to use this God-given capacity. Problems arise when people use reasoning alone to discern truth. According to this approach, if something cannot be scientifically investigated and proved, or if it cannot be philosophically solved, then it must not be truth.

Others trust emotional experience. To them, experience takes precedence over everything else.

According to this approach, if historical evidence fails to validate something or reasoning cannot verify it, their experience can determine the truth of it anyway. Using this approach, one might say, "But I know what I experienced."

Tradition is the third major way people determine truth. This includes church councils and denominational creeds. It also includes the philosophy "Well, this is what I have always been taught."

The fourth approach to determining truth is through and by the Scriptures. The cry of the Reformers was "Scripture alone." The reason for this emphasis was because the "Church" was dictating doctrine that was in opposition to Scripture. Many were defending the church's stance because of tradition, but the Reformers insisted that Scripture must take precedence over tradition. The church itself must be judged by Scripture. Our faith tradition must be judged by Scripture.

In a similar way, Scripture judges our experience. We must not be afraid to examine our experience in the light of Scripture. If the Bible contradicts the truthfulness of our experience, we must bow to Scripture. It is wonderful when our experience illustrates the Scriptures, and Scripture verifies the legitimacy of our experience.

If the Scriptures present something we cannot understand by reasoning, we must bow to truth as taught by Scripture. For example, it is impossible for us to grasp by reasoning that there is never a time that God is not, but we bow to the truth of the eternity of God as taught in Scripture.

Some things about being baptized in the Holy Spirit are hard to accept by reasoning alone. We cannot arrive at truth solely by what we have experienced or by what we have not experienced. Faith traditions set forth various statements of faith, some of which are contradictory. Therefore, they cannot all be true.

Our challenge is to pursue truth aggressively, persistently, receptively, sincerely and prayerfully. Sometimes truth hurts, and we grieve over the loss of what we thought was truth. Truth brings freedom, however.

Jesus said that the Holy Spirit will guide us into all truth (John 16:13). The Holy Spirit guided the human writers who wrote the Scriptures. He wants to help us in searching the Scriptures. He wants to help us in understanding, accepting and living by truth—giving priority to Scripture.

COMPLETE SUBMISSION

In Christian circles, we frequently speak of completely submitting our wills to Christ. Only then can we, as individuals and as a corporate group, become Christlike change agents in our world. If you have been part of a church for any length of time, this concept is probably familiar to you. Frequently overlooked in its presentation are the various dimensions of submission this necessarily includes.

Foundational to the submitting of our wills is the submission of all aspects of our lifestyles and beliefs to the Scriptures. The Bible doesn't give us specifics for every dimension and detail of the problems of life; however, it does give us principles we must learn to apply. To make these principles a part of our lifestyles, it is important to identify some things that can crowd our lives and cloud our perspective.

Ideas

Have you ever engaged a person in conversation when he or she expressed an outlandish idea? You may have thought, *That's the dumbest idea I've ever heard*! Perhaps you upgraded your inner response to *How could anyone come up with something like that?* How did you respond? In some cases you probably simply listened politely, then moved to another subject. In other situations, a noncommittal "Well, that's an interesting thought," comment seemed sufficient.

Wrong ideas may simply be a combination of various influences integrated in the mind without any analytical thinking. Or they may arise from someone's creative thinking or their sense of being an authority. Regardless of the source, however, the bottom line doesn't change. Personal ideas are being projected as truth. The dangers of this type of approach are too numerous to consider here. When it comes to belief and lifestyle, however, these ideas may be hazardous to one's spiritual health and in direct opposition to God's expressed truth. Plainly, the worst scenarios may lead to heresy. At the least, we may find ourselves living short of the fullness of the Spirit.

A large percentage of us are being influenced by a culture that has emphasized "self" for several decades. The overworked fast-food slogan "Have it your way" is a perspective far more dominant in our theology than we realize.

Our Experiences

"This is what happened to me!"

First-person testimony continues to be a powerful advertising strategy. Individuals share the message that using a particular product made (or makes) a difference in some dimension of their lives. Some are celebrities with "star" appeal; others are simply those with a story to tell of how their lives improved.

This thought brings us to an interesting crossroads: *To what extent can we base a truth on experience?* While some happenings are open to interpretation, depending on the personality and the situation, this relativity cannot be applied to all areas.

An example comes to mind. A sincere evangelical pastor's daughter began to have horrendous nightmares and exhibits unusual behavior, especially at night. Finding no immediate medical or psychological reasons for her behavior, the father began to entertain the possibility of believers being demon-possessed.

Spiritual experiences *are* a vital part of one's life in Christ! They speak to both our hearts and our minds. Experience in itself, however, cannot be presented as authoritative. Spiritual experiences must always be interpreted in light of the Scriptures' specific statements and guiding principles! Without this guide for interpretation, one can see the chaos that can easily arise. Soon a situation arises that is similar to the people of Israel in Judges 21:25. Each person merely does or believes according to his or her choice or experience.

Our Preferences

If the impacts of our personal preferences are overlooked, we will miss one of the realities of life. All of us favor, or lean to, a particular direction in the various areas of our lives. For some of us, we may be a "diehard" when it comes to the type and make of vehicle we drive. For others, critical preferences include clothing, recreational activities or art forms. Even when we aren't "hardcore" in an area, we still have our favorites . . . right? Sure we do!

Only a blah, disconnected person simply accepts anything without a sense of choice.

Preferences may also sneak into our Biblical and theological beliefs and views. Rather than committing to a careful study of Scripture and then coming to an informed conclusion, we may choose some other standard to guide us. This, of course, can easily be a false standard.

Occasionally you may hear someone say, "Let your conscience be your guide." This sounds good, but there are several big problems involved. *First, one's conscience doesn't automatically project a person to what is right and away from what is wrong.* Conscience reflects one's spiritual training and personal commitment to moral absolutes. These are conditioned and patterned by previous experience. Anytime these commitments are twisted, the conscience usually will produce a different set of results. For example, in some cultures stealing isn't wrong, but getting caught is!

Another problem with the concept of one's conscience being his guide rests in the subject matter. The conscience deals with moral issues; it does not cover all theological areas. The issue of speaking in tongues as the initial evidence of Spirit baptism is definitely not a moral decision. It is a theological decision that may impact one's total view and practice of spirituality; but it is not a matter of sinning or not sinning.

Preferences may steadily invade our belief structure because we do not want to be different from the majority or the prevailing thought patterns. Pause for a moment and be reminded that theology isn't a democracy. What the greater number of people believe and practice is not necessarily right. Spiritual renewal, Biblical orthodoxy and holy living never are trademarks of the masses. Even when solid Christian belief and practice advances, it is frequently the minority in the world that advances it. Sadly, this is true far too often within the church.

Preferences may push us in a particular direction in order to avoid difficult scenarios. We prefer an uncomplicated life of acceptability. This contrasts to early Pentecostals who held to their distinctive beliefs regardless of the disdain of a secular world and segments of the church. Probably they preferred not to experience some of the ridicule and suffering heaped on them because they embraced this new doctrine and practice. Undeterred, however, the various Pentecostal denominations held fast and made it possible for succeeding generations to experience the full gospel.

Our Comfort Zones

All comfort zones are not bad. When discussing spiritual issues and church problems, to be comfortable in a comfort zone is often pictured as negative.

This view needs to be reevaluated. We operate more efficiently when we are at ease with our surroundings and the particular actions required in an area. Most of us tend to fulfill our tasks to a better degree when we feel informed and capable. This is good, and we should strive for this attainment.

When it comes to Biblical truth, however, one's comfort zone will have to be disturbed if it conflicts with Scriptural truths and directives. To believe what others accept simply because we do not want to be different, or because we are unwilling to put forth the effort to explore, is an unacceptable posture. To do this means we are in submission to personal desire, rather than being submissive to the Word of God.

Our hope and prayer is that after reading and studying this book, you have been mentally and spiritually challenged to actively seek a Biblical perspective on speaking in tongues as the initial evidence of the baptism in the Holy Spirit. Know your current beliefs and understand why you hold them. We want you to be fully convinced you have adopted a doctrinal position that is in submission to the specifies of the Word of God!

STUDY GUIDE
Study Lesson 11

When you make a decision about your belief structure (what you believe), how do you go about coming to a final conclusion?

How much weight/impact do you give to the various influences such as opinions of others, personal experience, tradition and the Scriptures?

HISTORICAL PERSPECTIVE

We might be amazed at how little input is given to the process of coming to a conclusion about what we believe. There are some common responses which you probably recognize:

- "That's what my church or pastor believes."

- "My parents always said . . ."

- "All my friends are of the opinion . . ."

- "Well, it seems logical . . ."

Since what we believe may impact our spiritual future or our current spirituality and vitality in Christ, it seems like all of us would want to give careful thought as to how we have arrived at our current set of doctrinal beliefs and practices.

Look up Galatians 3:1 and write it in the space below.

_____

_____

The apostle Paul's rebuke of the Galatians was the sharpest language he used in writing to any of the believers. It is because they had truth but chose to listen to others who led them into doctrinal error.

STUDY QUESTIONS

1. What is the challenge each believer faces?

2. List the four approaches which usually are taken to determine truth.

3. How are we to pursue truth (five adjectives are given)?

4. What is the foundation for submitting our wills to Christ?

5. List the four elements which may cloud one's perspective of truth.

6. What are several sources for one's personal ideas?

7. How do we balance spiritual experiences so they do not become our authority?

8. Why should we be careful of the concept "Let your conscience be your guide"?

9. What are several reasons why we may allow preferences to guide our belief and practice?

10. When can a "comfort zone" be good?

PERSONAL PERSPECTIVE

It's so easy to personally develop an opinion or adopt another person's view as truth. But the value of these views is determined by their correlation with Scriptures. Human intelligence is God-given and of tremendous value to our overall living. It is, however, always to be subject to God's truth in Scripture.guide"?

Part V

Spirit Fullness

Receiving the Baptism in the Holy Spirit

A TESTIMONY

On a recent Sunday morning after worship, Mark said to me, "Pastor, I need to be baptized in the Holy Spirit. I need the power. If I'm going to be ministering to people in prison, I need the power of the Holy Spirit."

Mark and his wife, both from England, had been in the United States of America for a few months. He is planning to be a chaplain. We had talked about the need to be baptized in the Holy Spirit, and he had heard several sermons concerning the provisions. As God dealt with him, Mark began reading the Book of Joel, John 14—16, and the Book of Acts. He became convinced of the

211

necessity of the baptism in the Holy Spirit. Mark further stated, "This week I'm going to stop watching television and I'm going to concentrate on the Lord. Can you meet and pray with me one day?" I said, "Sure, let's meet Tuesday at 2 p.m.."

On Tuesday, Mark and I met at the church, and he told me of the problems that had arisen that day and the things that almost hindered his coming. Soon we started praying and worshiping the Lord. There was no music, no fanfare, no hype. It was not boisterous or demanding. We just enjoyed the presence of God as we praised and glorified God. Mark was baptized in the Holy Spirit and began to speak words he had never heard before—words given to him by the Holy Spirit. After a while of speaking in tongues and praising and magnifying God, Mark sat down on the front pew. He said, "I've never experienced anything like this. . . . This is indescribable. . . . I felt like a river was being poured out upon me, but I was not drowning."

As we have seen in our study, the Holy Spirit baptism is a gift from God for Christian believers. This gift is never earned nor deserved. We do not dictate the time nor the circumstances in which the gift is received. We do, however, cooperate with God so we can become ready to receive His gift. Some receive when hands are laid upon them. Some receive while the Word is being proclaimed. Some receive while praying and praising.

OBEYING

"And we are His witnesses to these things, and so also is the Holy Spirit whom God has given to those who obey Him" (Acts 5:32). Jesus said, "If you love Me, keep My commandments. And I will pray the Father, and He will give you another Helper, that He may abide with you forever" (John 14:15, 16).

So, check your obedience! Jesus had said to His disciples, "Behold the promise of the Father is upon you, but wait in the city until you are clothed upon with power from on high" (see Luke 24:49). One hundred twenty of these disciples obeyed and returned to Jerusalem and praised and prayed in the Upper Room for 10 days, obeying what Jesus said. According to 1 Corinthians 15:6, the resurrected Jesus appeared to more than 500 brothers and sisters at once; and yet, according to Acts 1:15, there were only about 120 who followed through in obedience in that gathering. Those obedient ones, who were still there when the Day of Pentecost arrived, were baptized in the Holy Spirit.

Saul had to obey and go into the city to be ready to receive the Holy Spirit baptism. Cornelius had to obey and send for Simon Peter and get ready to receive the Holy Spirit baptism. No amount of praying, fasting, emotional hype or positive reinforcement will take the place of obedience. "Be careful then how you live, not as unwise people but as wise, making the most of the time, because the days are evil. So do not be foolish, but understand what the will of the Lord is" (Ephesians 5:15-17, *NRSV*).

The will of the Lord includes sanctification or purity of life. Are there evidences of His sanctifying work in our lives? Drawing upon His sanctifying grace enables us to obey. This is the opportunity to check our relationship to the Lord. Is He truly Lord and Master of our lives, or are there any competing allegiances in our lives? God wants to prompt us concerning any areas to which we need to give attention. While we resist inordinate guilt from the Enemy, we appreciate and accept the Holy Spirit's reproving us, or convincing us, of things that hinder our relationship to God.

HUNGERING

Some have a take-it-or-leave-it attitude. Some assume that if this is for them, God will give it. Some are inconsistent in their desire. Allow God to help you to become *convinced of the necessity* of the baptism in the Holy Spirit. "Blessed are those who hunger and thirst for righteousness, for they shall be filled" (Matthew 5:6).

Jesus operated in Holy Spirit fullness. If we are to continue the works of Jesus, it is imperative that we operate in Holy Spirit fullness. *We desperately need the power of the Holy Spirit.*

EXPECTING

We must become *convinced that the baptism in the Holy Spirit is for us.* "For the promise is for you, for your children, and for all who are far away, everyone whom the Lord our God calls to him" (Acts 2:39, *NRSV*). If you have been birthed into the family of God by the Holy Spirit, this Holy Spirit baptism is available to you.

After the ascension of Jesus Christ, the disciples returned to Jerusalem with great joy and they went to the Upper Room and continued to worship in praise and praying. They did not know how long the wait would be, but they expected the promise to be fulfilled. What a tragedy if some would have given up on the ninth day and would have missed the occurrence on the 10th day!

Satan sometimes tries to dull our expectation with a feeling of disappointment. When we have prayed for this new vista of spirituality and nothing seemed to happen, how do we respond? We need to remind ourselves that our time in the presence of God is not wasted. We need to remind ourselves of God's promise, "Draw near to God and He will draw near to you" (James 4:8).

Be assured that when you conscientiously and intentionally draw near to God, you are getting closer to this experience, because God is drawing nearer to you. So instead of allowing yourself to become discouraged, praise God that He has drawn you closer and *keep on expecting to be baptized in the Holy Spirit.*

TRUSTING

Learning to trust God fully is imperative in being baptized in the Holy Spirit. "And without faith it is impossible to please God, for whoever would approach him must believe that he exists and that he rewards those who seek him" (Hebrews 11:6, *NRSV*). God is eternally faithful! His promises are YES and AMEN; no equivocating, no vacillating, no backing away from His promises. We can trust Him fully!

Jesus said: "So I say to you, Ask, and it will be given to you; seek, and you will find; knock, and it will be opened to you. For everyone who asks receives, and he who seeks finds, and to him who knocks it will be opened. If a son asks for bread from any father among you, will he give him a stone? Or if he asks for a fish, will he give him a serpent instead of a fish? Or if he asks for an egg, will he offer him a scorpion? If you then, being evil, know how to give good gifts to your children, how much more will your heavenly Father give the Holy Spirit to those who ask Him!" (Luke 11:9-13).

We, limited as we are in our understanding, would not respond to a request from our child in a way that would mock, frighten or endanger. God, who is all-loving and all-wise, certainly would outdo us. He will always grant the request appropriately. We can trust God completely that when we ask to be baptized in the Holy Spirit, that request will be granted.

WORSHIPING

There are variations in posture (kneeling, standing, sitting, etc.) and procedure (laying on of hands, corporate prayer, etc.), but the constant is that individuals are baptized in the Holy Spirit in an atmosphere of worship. You don't have to keep on begging God. Learn to relax and enjoy His presence. Praise and magnify the name of the Lord. Worship with expectation and anticipation. Don't try to impress God or others by your words. Just genuinely communicate with Almighty God. Don't depend on faddish approaches or certain human personalities, but cultivate your relationship to God and depend fully upon Him. Worship, worship, worship—with the gathered congregation, in the car, at home, with a small trusted prayer group. God is seeking worshipers who worship genuinely and according to truth.

LINGERING

Lingering or waiting in His presence is important. Many times we want instant results and instant answers, but God is Sovereign, and He does not operate on our time schedule. Some people say, "You don't have to tarry or wait!" Well, let's consider that statement. It is true that waiting does not earn God's blessing. It is true that we should not postpone what God wants to do in a moment. It is true that we should be urgent and expecting. However, the Sovereign Lord, the One in charge, knows what each needs and when.

Sometimes in our lingering in God's presence, He is teaching us, training us, nurturing us, growing us. If He granted our request immediately, we may never learn to appreciate His presence as we should; we may never learn to pray as we should; we may never learn to hunger for God as we should; we may never learn to check our motives, attitudes and actions as carefully as we should. Hopefully, in our lingering in His presence, we learn to put aside distractions and focus on God.

SUBMITTING

Submitting completely to God is a willingness to surrender our total being to be immersed in the Holy Spirit. We cultivate a receptivity to God's fullness rather than resisting. When we trust God fully, we do not have to fear receiving something erroneous. We can gladly and freely yield to God's Spirit. We are willing to submit even the tongue to become an instrument of divine praise with words which are strange to us, but words supplied by the Holy Spirit. James said that the tongue is an unruly member of the body that is hard to be tamed (James 3). It is the last bastion of control that we are willing to hand over to God. We may wonder how the words will sound or what others will think, but these concerns are laid aside as we begin to speak as the Holy Spirit guides us in what to say.

Receptivity . . . listen to Cornelius . . . and note the results. " 'So now all of us are here in the presence of God to listen to all that the Lord has commanded you to say.' . . . While Peter was still speaking, the Holy Spirit fell upon all who heard the word . . . for they heard them speaking in tongues and extolling God" (Acts 10:33, 44, 46, *NRSV*).

May God guide you in receiving and living in the fullness of His Holy Spirit!?

STUDY GUIDE
Study Lesson 12

QUESTIONS THAT WILL ASSIST YOUR PUR-
SUIT OF HOLY SPIRIT FULLNESS

1. Looking again at the component discussed, where am I in relationship to each?

2. Am I really convinced of the necessity of being baptized in the Holy Spirit?

3. Even though none of us deserves this marvelous gift, am I convinced that this Holy Spirit fullness is for me?

4. Am I cultivating a hungering and thirsting for God, not just for an experience?

5. Are there areas of obedience to which I need to give attention? (Be specific.)

6. Am I willing to spend time in God's presence to cultivate the relationship with Him and simply to enjoy His presence?

7. Am I afraid to speak forth strange words because I'm not sure whether this is really prompted by the Holy Spirit?

8. Do I trust God enough to know He will protect me from an alien spirit or from my own

imagination? Am I willing to submit myself to God fully, not just for an experience, but for a life of power, lived out fully in His will?

9. Am I willing to submit fully to God, even the last unruly member, my tongue, to speak forth what the Holy Spirit prompts me to say?

10. After being baptized in the Holy Spirit, am I willing to "keep on being filled," so mine is a lifestyle of Holy Spirit fullness?

11. Am I willing to help gently and respectfully a brother or sister in Christ to receive the fullness of the Spirit?